(England) Nottingham

Royal Charters Granted to the Burgesses of Nottingham, A.D.

1155-1712

(England) Nottingham

Royal Charters Granted to the Burgesses of Nottingham, A.D. 1155-1712

ISBN/EAN: 9783337161446

Printed in Europe, USA, Canada, Australia, Japan

Cover: Foto ©ninafisch / pixelio.de

More available books at **www.hansebooks.com**

ROYAL CHARTERS

GRANTED TO THE

BURGESSES OF NOTTINGHAM.

ROYAL CHARTERS

GRANTED TO THE

BURGESSES OF NOTTINGHAM

A.D. 1155—1712

ISSUED BY ORDER OF THE CORPORATION OF NOTTINGHAM

LONDON: BERNARD QUARITCH, 15, PICCADILLY
NOTTINGHAM: THOMAS FORMAN & SONS
M DCCC XC.

NOTTINGHAM:
THOS. FORMAN AND SONS, PRINTERS.

CONTENTS.

	PAGE
PREFACE	vii
HENRY II., Charter of ...	2
JOHN, Earl of Mortain, Charter of	4
JOHN, Charter of	8
HENRY III., First Charter of ...	12
HENRY III., Second Charter of	14
HENRY III., Third Charter of	16
EDWARD I., Charter of	18
EDWARD II., Charter of ...	22
EDWARD III., Charter of	26
EDWARD III., Letters Patent of, regarding election of Sheriffs...	32
RICHARD II., Grant of Fair	34
RICHARD II., Charter of ...	36
HENRY IV., Charter of	38
HENRY V., Charter of	48
HENRY VI., Charter of	48
EDWARD IV., Charter of ...	72
HENRY VII., Charter of	72
HENRY VIII., Charter of...	74
EDWARD VI., Charter of ...	76
PHILIP AND MARY, Charter of ...	78
ELIZABETH, Charter of ...	80
JAMES I., Charter of	82
JAMES I., Exemplification of Charter of Henry VI., by ...	84
CHARLES I., Charter of	84
CHARLES II., Charter of	86
JAMES II., Charter of	122
WILLIAM AND MARY, Charter of	128
ANNE, Grant of two Fairs by	140

PREFACE.

The privileges and immunities conferred upon the Burgesses of Nottingham by the Kings of England are so numerous that it is necessary for legal purposes to make frequent reference to the various charters by which these privileges were conferred. Hence it is desirable that accurate texts and translations of these charters should be available. This want has been partly met by the printing of the charters up to 1625 in the *Records of the Borough of Nottingham*, of which four volumes have been issued by the Corporation. As, however, reference to the charters spread over four volumes is not very easy, and as several of the charters still required to be edited and translated, the Finance Committee of the Corporation authorized the preparation of the present volume, which gives in a convenient form texts and translations of the whole of the royal charters. The volume includes the charters of Charles II. and James II., which are published for the first time. These charters were cancelled by William and Mary, but they are here published as they are historically of interest as illustrating the attacks made upon municipal privileges by the last two Stuart monarchs. The charter of Charles II. possesses a further interest, for it records modes of government, etc., that had grown up in the town since the date of the charter of Henry VI.

An exhaustive analytical index of the contents of the charters has been added with a view of facilitating reference.

The work has been prepared by Mr. W. H. STEVENSON, by whom the *Records* were edited.

SAM. GEO. JOHNSON,
Town Clerk.

GUILDHALL, NOTTINGHAM.
July 31st, 1890.

ROYAL CHARTERS OF LIBERTIES

GRANTED TO THE

BURGESSES OF NOTTINGHAM.

ROYAL CHARTERS OF LIBERTIES

GRANTED TO THE

BURGESSES OF NOTTINGHAM.

I.—*Charter of King Henry II.*
[1155—1165.]

HENRY II.

¹H[ENRICUS,] Rex Angliae, et Dux Normanniae et Aquitanniae, et Comes Andegaviae, archiepiscopis, episcopis, comitibus, baronibus, justitiariis, vicecomitibus, ministris, et omnibus fidelibus suis, Francis et Anglis, totius Angliae, salutem.

Confirms customs enjoyed in time of Henry I.

Sciatis me concessisse, et hac mea carta confirmasse, Burgensibus de Noting[ham] omnes illas liberas consuetudines, quas habuerunt tempore Regis Henrici avi mei; scilicet, *Tol* et *Theam*, et *Infangenethcof*, et Thelonea a Thurmotestona usque ad Newerc', et de omnibus Trentam transcuntibus, ita plenarie ut in burgo de Noting[ham]; et ex alia parte a duito ultra Rempestunam usque ad aquam de Radeford in Nort.

Toll on the Trent.

Market on Friday and Saturday.

Homines etiam de Noting[ham]scir' et de Derbisir' venire debent ad burgum de Noting[ham] die Veneris et Sabbati, cum quadrigis et summagiis suis.

Dyeing of cloth restricted to town.

Nec aliquis infra decem leucas in circuitu de Noting[ham] tinctos pannos operari debet, nisi in burgo de Notingh[am].

Freedom gained by year's residence in town.

Et si aliquis, undecunque sit, in burgo de Noting[ham] manserit anno uno et die uno, tempore pacis, absque calumpnia, nullus postea nisi rex in eum jus habebit.

Burgesses to possess land after peaceful enjoyment of a year and day.

Et quicunque burgensium terram vicini sui emerit, et possederit per annum integrum et diem unum, absque calumpnia parentum vendentis, si in Anglia fuerint, postea eam quiete possidebit.

The reeve cannot prosecute except when another burgess is prosecutor.

Neque praeposito burgi de Notingh[am] aliquem burgensium calumpnianti respondeatur, nisi alius fuerit accusator in causa.

¹ This charter has been printed from an enrolment among the Government records, in Rymer's *Foedera*, ed. 1816, i. 41, and from thence in Prof. Stubbs' *Select Charters*, p. 166.

ROYAL CHARTERS OF LIBERTIES

GRANTED TO THE

BURGESSES OF NOTTINGHAM.

I.—*Charter of King Henry II.*
[1155—1165.]

¹HENRY, King of England, and Duke of Normandy and Aquitaine, and Earl of Anjou, to his archbishops, bishops, earls, barons, justiciaries, sheriffs, ministers, and all his faithful subjects, French and English, of all England, greeting. *HENRY II.*

Know ye that I have granted, and by this my charter have confirmed, to the Burgesses of Nottingham all those free customs which they had in the time of King Henry my grandfather; to wit, Tol and Theam, and Infangenetheof, and Thelonea from Thrumpton to Newark, and of all things crossing the Trent, as fully as in the borough of Nottingham; and on the other side from the brook beyond Rempston to the water of Retford in the north. *Confirms customs enjoyed in time of Henry I. Toll on the Trent.*

Moreover, the men of Nottinghamshire and Derbyshire ought to come to the borough of Nottingham on Friday and Saturday, with their wains and packhorses. *Market on Friday and Saturday.*

Nor ought any one within a radius of ten *leucae* of Nottingham to work dyed cloths, except in the borough of Nottingham. *Dyeing of cloth restricted to town.*

And if any one, whencesoever he may be, shall dwell in the borough of Nottingham a year and a day, in time of peace, without claim, no one afterwards except the king shall have any right in him. *Freedom gained by year's residence in town.*

And whosoever of the burgesses shall buy the land of his neighbour, and shall possess it for a whole year and a day, without claim on the part of the kindred of the vendor, if they be in England, he shall afterwards quietly possess it. *Burgesses to possess land after peaceful enjoyment of a year and day.*

Nor shall it be answered to the reeve of the borough of Nottingham challenging any burgess, unless another shall be the plaintiff in the case. *The reeve cannot prosecute except when another burgess is prosecutor.*

Residents in borough to contribute to tallages, etc.

Et quicunque in burgo manserit, cujuscunque feodi sit, reddere debet simul cum burgensibus taillagia, et defectus burgi adimplere.

Freedom for those attending market.

Omnes etiam qui ad forum de Notingh[am] venerint a vespere diei Veneris usque ad vesperam Sabbati, non namientur, nisi pro firma regis.

Passage of Trent to be free.

Et iter de Trenta liberum esse debet navigantibus quantum pertica una optinebit ex utraque parte fili aquae.

Quare volo et firmiter praecipio, quod praedicti Burgenses praedictas consuetudines habeant et teneant bene et in pace, et libere, et quiete, et honorifice, et plenarie, et integre, sicut habuerunt tempore Regis H[enrici] avi mei.

Testibus: Ricardo de Hum[et,] Conest[abulario]; Willelmo de Braosio; Willelmo de Caisneto; Willelmo de Lanvalei; Rann[ulfo,] Vic[ecomite] de Noting[ham].[1] Apud Eborac[um].

4151.

II.—*Charter of John, Earl of Mortain, confirming the Charter of his father, King Henry II.*

[*Circa* 1189.]

John, Earl of Mortain.

[2][JOHANNES, Comes] Moret[oniae], omnibus hominibus et amicis suis, Francis et Anglis, praesentibus et futuris, salutem.

Sciatis me concessisse, et hac praesenti carta mea confirmasse, Burgensibus meis Notingeham', omnes illas liberas consuetudines, quas habuerunt tempore Henrici Regis, proavi mei, et tempore Henrici Regis, patris mei, sicut carta ejusdem Henrici patris mei testatur:

Recital of charter of Henry II.

Scilicet, *Thol* et *Theam*, et *Infangenetheof*, et Tholonea, a Thurmodeston' usque ad Niwerch', et de omnibus Trentam transeuntibus, ita plenarie ut in burgo de Notingeham; et ex alia parte a duitto ultra Rempeston' usque ad aquam de Radeford in Nord', et de Bikeresdic.[3]

Homines etiam de Notingehamsir' et de Derbisir' venire debent ad burgum de Notingeham die Veneris et Sabbati, cum quadrigis et summagiis suis.

[1] Ranulf son of Ingelram was Sheriff of Notts. and Derby from 2 Hen. II. to 11 Hen. II. This charter was most probably granted early in 1155, when Henry visited York and Nottingham. See Prof. Stubbs' *Outline Itinerary of Hen. II*, in Chron. of Benedict Abbas, ii. p. cxxix.

And whosoever shall dwell in the borough, of whatsoever fee he may be, he ought to pay tallages together with the burgesses, and make up the deficiencies of the borough.

Residents in borough to contribute to tallages, etc.

Also all who come to the market of Nottingham from the eve of Friday to the eve of Saturday, shall not be distrained, except for the King's ferm.

Freedom for those attending market.

And the passage of the Trent ought to be free to navigators as far as one perch extends on either side of the mid-stream.

Passage of Trent to be free.

Wherefore I will and firmly enjoin that the aforesaid Burgesses shall have and hold the said customs in good manner and in peace, and freely and quietly, and honourably, and fully, and wholly, as they had in the time of King Henry my grandfather.

Witnesses: Richard de Humet, Constable; William de Braose; William de Caisneto; William de Lanvalei; Ranulf, Sheriff of Nottingham.[1] At York. 4151.

II.—*Charter of John, Earl of Mortain, confirming the Charter of his father, King Henry II.*

[*Circa* 1189.]

[2]JOHN, Earl of Mortain, to all his men and friends, French and English, present and to come, greeting.

John, Earl of Mortain.

Know ye that I have granted, and by this my present charter have confirmed, to my Burgesses of Nottingham all those free customs which they had in the time of King Henry, my great-grandfather, and in the time of King Henry, my father, as the charter of the same Henry my father witnesses:

To wit, Thol and Theam, and Infangenetheof, and Tholonea, from Thrumpton to Newark, and of everything crossing the Trent, as fully as in the borough of Nottingham; and on the other side from the brook beyond Rempston to the water of Retford in the north, and from Bycardyke.

Recital of charter of Henry II.

Also the men of Nottinghamshire and Derbyshire ought to come to the borough of Nottingham on Friday and Saturday, with their wains and pack-horses.

---

[2] This Charter has never before been printed, as it has been overshadowed by John's subsequent Charter as King. Richard I. conferred the town upon John in 1189; Chron. of Benedict Abbas, ii. 78.

[3] Now known as 'Bycardyke,' the northern boundary of the county.

John, Earl of Mortain.

Nec aliquis infra decem leucas in circuitu de Notingeham tinctos pannos operari debet, nisi in burgo de Notingeham.

Et si aliquis, undecunque sit, in burgo de Notingeham manserit uno anno et die uno, tempore pacis et absque calumpnia, nullus postea, nisi ego, in eum jus habebit.

Et quicumque burgensium terram vicini sui emerit, et possederit per annum integrum et diem unum absque calumpnia parentum vendentis, si in Anglia fuerint, postea eam quiete possidebit.

Neque praeposito burgi de Notingeham aliquem burgensium calumpnianti respondeatur, nisi alius fuerit accusator in causa.

Et quicunque [in burgo ma]nserit, cujuscunque feodi sit, reddere debet simul cum burgensibus tailagia, et defectus burgi adimplere.

Omnes etiam qui [ad forum] de Notingeham venerint a vespere die[i] Veneris usque ad vesperam Sabbati, non namientur nisi pro firma mea.

Et iter de Trente [liberum] esse debet navigantibus quantum pertica una optinebit ex utraque parte fili aquae.

Grant of a Gild Merchant.

Praeterea concessi etiam, de proprio dono meo, et hac mea [carta] confirmavi eisdem liberis Burgensibus meis, Gildam Mercatorum, cum omnibus libertatibus et liberis consuetudinibus, quae ad Gildam Mercatorum debent [vel sole]nt pertinere.

Burgesses to be quit of tolls.

Et quod ipsi sint quieti de Tholonea per totam terram meam, infra nundinas et extra.

They may appoint a Reeve from themselves, removable at John's pleasure.

Et licet illis quem voluerint ex suis in fine anni praepositum suum facere, qui de firma mea pro ipsis respondeat; ita quod si idem praepositus mihi displiceat, illum ad voluntatem meam removebo, et ipsi alium ad libitum meum substituent.

The Reeve so elected to pay the fee-farm of the Borough into John's Exchequer.

Concessi etiam eisdem Burgensibus, ut quicunque ab eis constitutus fuerit praepositus ejusdem burgi, solvat firmam ejusdem burgi ad dominicum scaccarium meum, ubicunque fuerit in Anglia, ad duos terminos, medietatem, scilicet, ad clausum Paschae, et medietatem in octavis Sancti Michaëlis.

Enactment clause.

Quare volo et firmiter praecipio, quod praedicti Burgenses habeant et teneant praedictas consuetudines bene et in pace, libere et quiete, honorifice et pacifice, plenarie et integre, sicut habuerunt tempore Henrici Regis, proavi mei, et tempore Henrici Regis, patris mei, cum praedictis augmentis, quae eis

Nor ought any one to work dyed cloths within a radius of ten *leucae* of Nottingham, except in the borough of Nottingham.

<small>John, Earl of Mortain.</small>

And if any one, whencesoever he may be, shall dwell in the borough of Nottingham a year and a day, in time of peace, and without claim, no one afterwards, but I, shall have any right in him.

And whosoever of the burgesses shall buy the land of his neighbour, and shall possess it for a whole year and a day without claim by the kindred of the vendor, if they be in England, he shall afterwards quietly possess it.

Nor shall it be answered to the reeve of Nottingham challenging any of the burgesses, unless another shall be the plaintiff in the case.

And whosoever shall dwell in [the borough], of whatsoever fee he may be, he ought to pay tallages together with the burgesses, and make good the deficiencies of the borough.

Also all who shall come [to the market] of Nottingham from the eve of Friday to the evening of Saturday shall not be distrained except for my ferm.

And the passage of Trent ought to be free to navigators as far as one perch extends on either side of the mid-stream.

Moreover, I have also granted, of my own gift, and by this my [charter] have confirmed to the same my free Burgesses, a Merchants' Gild, with all the liberties and free customs which should, or do usually belong to a Merchants' Gild.

<small>Grant of a Gild Merchant.</small>

And that they shall be quit of Tholonea throughout the whole of my land, within and without fairs.

<small>Burgesses to be quit of tolls.</small>

And they may make, at the end of the year, whom they will from amongst themselves their reeve, who shall answer on their behalf for my ferm; provided that if the same reeve shall displease me, I shall remove him at my will, and they shall substitute another at my pleasure.

<small>They may appoint a Reeve from themselves, removable at John's pleasure.</small>

Also I have granted to the same Burgesses that whosoever shall be constituted reeve of the same borough, shall pay the ferm of the same borough to my demesne exchequer, wherever it may be in England, at two terms, to wit, a moiety at the close of Easter, and a moiety in the octave of Saint Michael.

<small>The Reeve so elected to pay the feeferm of the borough into John's Exchequer.</small>

Wherefore I will and firmly enjoin that the aforesaid Burgesses shall have and hold the aforesaid customs well and in peace, freely and quietly, honourably and peacefully, fully and wholly, as they had them in the time of King Henry, my great-grandfather, and in the time of King Henry, my father, with

<small>Enactment clause.</small>

concessi. Et prohibeo, ne quis contra hanc cartam meam praedictos Burgenses vexare praesumat in aliquo, super decem libras forisfacti mei.

Hiis testibus: Hugone, Coventrensi Episcopo; Ada, Abbate de Wellebec; Alexandro, Priore de Lenton'; Aldr[edo,] Priore de Novo Loco; Rogero de Play'; Girardo de Canvill; Henrico de Ver; Radulfo Murdac; Galfrido de Jorz; Samsone de Stretlee; Simone, filio Ricardi; Roberto de Fornellis; Willelmo de Furnellis; Willelmo de Craumunt; Rogero de Karkeny'; Galfrido Luterell'; Magistro Benedicto; Serlone clerico; et multis aliis. 4152.

III.—*Charter of King John, confirming grants made by him whilst Earl of Mortain.*

1199-1200, March 19.

[1]JOHANNES, Dei gratia, Rex Angliae, Dominus Hyberniae, Dux Normanniae, Aquitanniae, et Comes Andegaviae, archiepiscopis, episcopis, abbatibus, comitibus, baronibus, justitiariis, vicecomitibus, et omnibus ballivis et fidelibus suis totius Angliae, salutem.

Sciatis nos concessisse, et praesenti carta nostra confirmasse, Burgensibus nostris de Notingeham omnes illas liberas consuetudines, quas habuerunt tempore Henrici Regis, proavi nostri, et tempore Henrici Regis, patris nostri, sicut carta ejusdem Henrici patris nostri testatur:

Scilicet, *Thol* et *Theam*, et *Infangenetheof*, et Tholonea a Thurmodeston' usque ad Niwerk, et de omnibus Trentam transeuntibus, ita plenarie ut in burgo de Notingham; et ex alia parte a duitto ultra Rempeston' usque ad aquam de Radeford in Nord',
et de Bikeresdik.

Homines etiam de Notinghamsir' et de Derebisir' venire debent ad burgum de Notingham die Veneris et Sabbati, cum quadrigis et summagiis suis.

Nec aliquis infra decem leucas in circuitu de Notingham tinctos pannos operari debet, nisi in burgo de Notingham.

Et si aliquis, undecunque sit, in burgo de Notingham manserit uno anno et die uno, tempore pacis et absque calumpnia, nullus postea nisi Rex in eum jus habebit.

---

[1] This charter has been printed in the Charter Rolls of John, p. 39, and from thence in Stubbs' *Select Charters*, p. 308.

the aforesaid augmentations which I have granted them. And JOHN.
I forbid that any one presume to vex the said Burgesses in
aught against this my charter, upon pain of ten pounds to be
forfeited to me.

These being witnesses: Hugh, Bishop of Coventry; Adam,
Abbot of Welbeck; Alexander, Prior of Lenton; Aldred, Prior
of Newstead; Roger de Play'; Gerard de Camville; Henry de
Vere; Ralph Murdac; Geoffrey de Jorz; Sampson de Strelley;
Simon Fitz-Richard; Robert de Furneux; William de Furneux;
William de Craumunt; Roger de Karkeny; Geoffrey Luterel;
Master Benedict; Serlo the clerk; and many others. 4152.

III.—*Charter of King John, confirming grants made by him whilst Earl of Mortain.*

1199-1200, March 19.

¹JOHN, by the grace of God, King of England, Lord of JOHN.
Ireland, Duke of Normandy, Aquitaine, and Earl of Anjou, to
his archbishops, bishops, abbots, earls, barons, justiciaries,
sheriffs, and bailiffs and faithful subjects of all England,
greeting.

Know ye that we have granted, and by our present charter Recital of
have confirmed, to our Burgesses of Nottingham, all those free charter of
customs which they had in the time of King Henry, our great- Henry II.
grandfather, and in the time of King Henry, our father, as the
charter of the same Henry our father witnesses:

To wit, Thol and Theam, and Infangentheof, and Tholonea from
Thrumpton to Newark, and of all things passing the Trent, as fully
as in the borough of Nottingham; and on the other side from the
brook beyond Rempston to the water of Retford in the North,
and from Bycardyke.

Also the men of Nottinghamshire and Derbyshire ought to come to
the borough of Nottingham on Friday and Saturday with their wains
and pack-horses.

Nor ought any one to work dyed cloths within a radius of ten *leucae*
of Nottingham, except in the borough of Nottingham.

And if any one, whencesoever he may be, shall remain in Nottingham
a year and a day, in time of peace, and without claim, no one afterwards
except the King shall have any right in him.

JOHN.

Et quicumque burgensium terram vicini sui emerit, et possederit per annum integrum et diem unum, absque calumpnia parentum vendentis, si in Anglia fuerint, postea eam quiete possidebit.

Neque praeposito burgi de Notingham aliquem burgensium calumpnianti respondeatur, nisi alius fuerit accusator in causa.

Et quicunque in burgo manserit, cujuscunque feodi sit, reddere debet simul cum burgensibus taillagia, et defectus burgi adimplere.

Omnes etiam, qui ad forum de Notingham venerint a vespere die[i] Veneris usque ad vesperam Sabbati, non namientur, nisi pro firma nostra.

Et iter de Trente liberum esse debet navigantibus quantum pertica una optinebit ex utraque parte fili aquae.

Grant of a Gild Merchant.

Praeterea concessimus etiam, de proprio dono nostro, et hac carta nostra confirmavimus, eisdem liberis Burgensibus nostris Gildam Mercatorum, cum omnibus libertatibus et liberis consuetudinibus, quae ad Gildam Mercatorum debent vel solent pertinere.

Burgesses to be quit of tolls.

Et quod ipsi sint quieti de Tholonea per totam terram nostram, infra nundinas et extra.

They may appoint a Reeve from themselves, removable at Royal pleasure.

Et licet illis quem voluerint ex suis in fine anni praepositum suum facere, qui de firma nostra pro ipsis respondeat; ita quod si idem praepositus nobis displiceat, illum ad voluntatem nostram removebimus, et ipsi alium ad libitum nostrum substituent.

The Reeve so elected to pay the fee-ferm of the Borough into the Exchequer.

Concessimus etiam eisdem Burgensibus, ut quicumque ab eis constitutus fuerit praepositus ejusdem burgi, solvat firmam ejusdem burgi ad dominicum scaccarium nostrum, ubicunque fuerit in Anglia, ad duos terminos, medietatem, scilicet, ad clausum Paschae, et medietatem in octabis Sancti Michaëlis.

Quare volumus et firmiter praecipimus, quod praedicti Burgenses habeant et teneant praedictas consuetudines, bene et in pace, libere et quiete, honorifice et pacifice, plenarie et integre, sicut habuerunt tempore Henrici Regis, proavi nostri, et tempore Henrici Regis, patris nostri, cum praedictis augmentis, quae eis concessimus. Et prohibemus, ne quis contra hanc cartam nostram praedictos Burgenses vexare praesumat in aliquo, super decem libras forisfacti nostri, sicut eis concessimus et rationabili carta nostra confirmavimus dum essemus Comes Moretoniae.

And whosoever of the burgesses shall buy the land of his neighbour, and shall possess it for a whole year and a day, without claim by the kindred of the vendor, if they be in England, he shall afterwards quietly possess it.

Nor shall it be answered to the reeve of Nottingham challenging any of the burgesses, unless another shall be the plaintiff in the case.

And whosoever shall dwell in the borough, of whatsoever fee he may be, ought to pay tallages, and make good the deficiencies of the borough.

Also all who shall come to the market of Nottingham from the eve of Friday to the evening of Saturday shall not be distrained, except for our ferm.

And the passage of Trent ought to be free to navigators as far as one perch extends on either side of the mid-stream.

Moreover, we have granted, of our own gift, and by this our present charter have confirmed, to the same our free Burgesses a Merchants' Gild, with all the liberties and free customs which should, or do usually pertain to a Merchants' Gild. *Grant of a Gild Merchant.*

And that they shall be quit of Tholonea throughout the whole of our land, within and without fairs. *Burgesses to be quit of tolls.*

And they may make, at the end of the year, whom they will from amongst themselves their reeve, who shall answer for our ferm on their behalf; provided that if the same reeve shall displease us, we shall remove him at our will, and they shall substitute another at our pleasure. *They may appoint a Reeve from themselves, removable at Royal pleasure.*

Also we have granted to the same Burgesses that whosoever shall be constituted reeve of the same borough, shall pay the ferm of the same borough at our demesne exchequer, wheresoever it may be in England, at two terms, to wit, a moiety at the close of Easter, and a moiety in the octave of Saint Michael. *The Reeve so elected to pay the fee-ferm of the Borough into the Exchequer.*

Wherefore we will and firmly enjoin, that the aforesaid Burgesses shall have and hold the aforesaid customs, well and in peace, freely and quietly, honourably and peacefully, fully and wholly, as they had in the time of King Henry, our great-grandfather, and in the time of King Henry, our father, with the aforesaid augmentations which we have granted them. And we forbid that any one presume to vex the aforesaid Burgesses in aught against this our charter, under pain of ten pounds to be forfeited to us, as we granted and by our reasonable charter confirmed when we were Earl of Mortain.

JOHN.

Hiis testibus: Gaufrido, filio Petri, Comite Essexiae; Willelmo Briwere; Hugone Bard[ulf]; Roberto, filio Rogeri; Willelmo de Stotevill'; Hugone de Nevill'; Simone de Pateshull'; Gilleberto de Norfolk.

Datum per manus Simonis, Archidiaconi Wellensis, et Johannis de Gray, Archidiaconi Clivelandiae, apud Clipston, xix. die Martii, regni nostri anno primo.   4153.

IV.—*First Charter of King Henry III.*
1229-30, February 24.

HENRY III. first charter.

HENRICUS, Dei gratia, Rex Angliae, Dominus Hyberniae, Dux Normanniae, Aquitanniae, et Comes Andegaviae, archiepiscopis, episcopis, abbatibus, prioribus, comitibus, baronibus, justitiariis, vicecomitibus, praepositis, ministris, et omnibus ballivis et fidelibus suis, salutem.

Confirmation of previous charters.

Inspeximus cartam Domini Johannis Regis, patris nostri, factam Burgensibus nostris Notingham, in haec verba: 'JOHANNES, Dei gratia,' [*etc., reciting King John's Charter, No. III.*]. Nos igitur, has donationes et concessiones ratas et gratas habentes, eas praedictis Burgensibus, pro nobis et heredibus nostris, concedimus et confirmamus.

The Burgesses may pay the ferm of the Borough directly into the Exchequer.

Praeterea, concessimus de proprio dono nostro, et hac carta nostra confirmamus, pro nobis et heredibus nostris, eisdem Burgensibus, et corum heredibus, quod praedictam firmam ejusdem burgi, videlicet, quinquaginta et duas libras *blanc*, reddant nobis, per manum suam, ad Scaccarium nostrum ad duos terminos, scilicet, viginti et sex libras ad Clausum Pascha, et viginti et sex libras in octabis Sancti Michaëlis; et quod ipsi et corum

May hold the Borough by the said fee-ferm.

heredes habeant et teneant praedictam villam per praedictam firmam quinquaginta duarum librarum *blanc*, sicut praedictum est.

They may take tronage of merchandise that is sold by weight.

Concessimus etiam, pro nobis et heredibus nostris, eisdem Burgensibus et heredibus suis, quod capiant tronagium in villa de Notingham de mercandisis quae consistunt in pondere, sicut capi consueverunt in aliis burgis nostris et civitatibus per Angliam.

May elect their Coroners.

Et quod habeant coronatores ex se ipsis in eadem villa.

Quare volumus et firmiter praecipimus, quod praedicti

These being witnesses: Geoffrey Fitz-Peter, Earl of Essex; John William Briwere; Hugh Bardolf; Robert Fitz-Roger; William de Stuteville; Hugh de Neville; Simon de Pateshull; Gilbert de Norfolk.

Given by the hands of Simon, Archdeacon of Wells, and John de Gray, Archdeacon of Cleveland, at Clipston, the 19th day of March, in the first year of our reign. 4153.

IV.—*First Charter of King Henry III.*
1229-30, February 24.

HENRY, by the grace of God, King of England, Lord of Ireland, Duke of Normandy, Aquitaine, and Earl of Anjou, to his archbishops, bishops, abbots, priors, earls, barons, justices, sheriffs, reeves, ministers, and all his bailiffs and faithful subjects, greeting. HENRY III. first charter.

We have inspected the charter of the Lord King John, our father, made to our Burgesses of Nottingham, in these words: 'JOHN, by the grace of God,' [*etc., reciting King John's Charter, No. III.*]. We, therefore, accounting these gifts and grants as valid and acceptable, do grant and confirm them to the aforesaid Burgesses for us and our heirs. Confirmation of previous charters.

Moreover, we have granted of our own gift, and by this our charter do confirm, for us and our heirs, to the same Burgesses, and their heirs, that they may render to us the aforesaid ferm of the same borough, to wit, fifty-two pounds blanc, by their hand at our Exchequer at two terms, to wit, twenty-six pounds at the Close of Easter, and twenty-six pounds in the octave of Saint Michael; and that they and their heirs may have and hold the aforesaid town by the aforesaid ferm of fifty-two pounds blank, as is aforesaid. The Burgesses may pay the ferm of the Borough directly into the Exchequer. May hold the Borough by the said ferm.

We have also granted, for us and our heirs, to the same Burgesses and their heirs, that they may take tronage in the town of Nottingham of wares which go by weight, as they are used to take in other our boroughs and cities throughout England. They may take tronage of merchandise that is sold by weight.

And that they may have coroners from themselves in the same town. May elect their Coroners.

Wherefore we will and firmly enjoin that the aforesaid

HENRY III.
Enactment clause.

Burgenses, et eorum heredes, habeant et teneant, de proprio dono nostro, libertates et consuetudines praedictas, bene et in pace, libere, quiete, et integre: videlicet, quod reddant nobis per manum suam singulis annis ad Scaccarium nostrum, ad duos terminos praedictos, praedictas quinquaginta et duas libras *blanc*; et quod ipsi, et eorum heredes, habeant et teneant praedictam villam per praedictam firmam quinquaginta et duarum librarum *blanc*; et quod ipsi capiant tronagium praedictum, et habeant coronatores ex se ipsis in eadem villa de Notingham', ut praedictum est.

Hiis testibus: Johanne Bathoniensi, R[icardo] Dunholmensi, Waltero Karleolensi, Episcopis; H[uberto] de Burgo, Comite Kantiae, Justitiario Angliae; Hugone de Nevill'; Galfrido de Luscy; Stephano de Sedgrave; Radulfo, filio Nicholai; Johanne, filio Philippi; Henrico de Capella; et aliis.

Datum per manum venerabilis patris R[adulfi], Cycestrensis Episcopi, Cancellarii nostri, apud Westmonasterium, vicesimo quarto die Februarii, anno regni nostri quarto decimo.   4154.

V.—Second Charter of King Henry III.

1255, July 20.

HENRY III.
second charter

[H]ENRICUS, Dei gratia, Rex Angliae, Dominus Hyberniae, Dux Normanniae, Aquitanniae, et Comes Andegaviae, archiepiscopis, episcopis, abbatibus, prioribus, comitibus, baronibus, justitiariis, vicecomitibus, praepositis, ministris, et omnibus ballivis et fidelibus suis, salutem.

The Burgesses shall not be arrested elsewhere for debts owing by other Burgesses;

Sciatis nos concessisse, et hac carta nostra confirmasse, Burgensibus nostris Notingham, quod ipsi, et eorum heredes, imperpetuum per totam terram et p[ote]statem nostram habeant hanc libertatem, videlicet, quod ipsi, vel eorum bona quocumque locorum in potestate nostra inventa, non arestentur pro aliquo debito de quo fidejussores aut principales debitores non exstiterint, nisi forte ipsi debitores de eorum sint communa et potestate,

unless they have failed to do justice to the creditors.

habentes unde de debitis suis in toto vel in parte satisfacere possint, et dicti Burgenses creditoribus eorumdem debitorum in justitia defuerint, et de hoc rationabiliter constare possit.

Grant of return of writs.

Concessimus etiam, et hac carta nostra confirmavimus, eisdem Burgensibus, quod imperpetuum habeant returnum

Burgesses, and their heirs, shall have and hold, of our own gift, the aforesaid liberties and customs, well and in peace, freely, quietly, and wholly: that is to say, that they shall render to us by their hand every year at our Exchequer, at the two terms aforesaid, the aforesaid fifty-two pounds blanc; and that they, and their heirs, shall have and hold the aforesaid town by the aforesaid ferm of fifty-two pounds blanc; and that they shall take the aforesaid tronage, and have coroners from themselves in the same town of Nottingham, as is aforesaid. HENRY III. Enactment clause.

These being witnesses: John, Bishop of Bath; Richard, Bishop of Durham; Walter, Bishop of Carlisle; Hubert de Burgh, Earl of Kent, Justiciary of England; Hugh de Nevill; Geoffrey de Lucy; Stephen de Segrave; Ralph Fitz-Nicholas; John Fitz-Philip; Henry de Capella; and others.

Given by the hand of the venerable father Ralph, Bishop of Chichester, our Chancellor, at Westminster, the twenty-fourth day of February, in the fourteenth year of our reign.   4154.

V.—*Second Charter of King Henry III.*
1255, July 20.

HENRY, by the grace of God, King of England, Lord of Ireland, Duke of Normandy and Aquitaine, and Earl of Anjou, to his archbishops, bishops, abbots, priors, earls, barons, justices, sheriffs, reeves, ministers, and all his bailiffs and faithful subjects, greeting. HENRY III. second charter

Know ye that we have granted, and by this our present charter have confirmed, to our Burgesses of Nottingham, that they, and their heirs, shall have for ever throughout our land and jurisdiction this liberty, that is to say, that they or their goods, in whatsoever places found within our jurisdiction, shall not be arrested for any debt of which they are not the pledges or principal debtors, except in case the debtors are of their commune and power, having whereof their debts may be wholly or partly satisfied, and the said Burgesses shall have failed in doing justice to the creditors of the same debtors, and that this can be reasonably made to appear. The Burgesses shall not be arrested elsewhere for debts owing by other Burgesses; unless they have failed to do justice to the creditors

We have also granted, and by this our charter have confirmed to the same Burgesses, that they shall have for ever the Grant of return of writs,

brevium nostrorum de summonitionibus Scaccarii nostri, de omnibus ad burgum nostrum Notingham' pertinentibus, ita quod nullus vicecomes, aut alius ballivus vel minister noster, decetero intromittat se de hujusmodi summonitionibus aut districtionibus faciendis in praedicto burgo, nisi per defectum dictorum Burgensium aut Ballivorum ejusdem burgi.

Enactment clause.

Quare volumus et firmiter praecipimus, pro nobis et heredibus nostris, quod praedicti Burgenses et eorum heredes imperpetuum habeant libertates praescriptas, sicut praedictum est. Et prohibemus, super forisfacturam nostram decem librarum, ne quis eos contra libertates illas in aliquo injuste vexet, disturbet, vel inquietet.

Hiis testibus: Rogero le Bigot, Comite Norf[olk'], Marescallo Angliae; Radulfo, filio Nicholai; Johanne de Lessinton'; Ricardo de Grey; Willelmo de Grey; Ymberto Poieys; Waukelino de Aerdern; Petro Everardi; Willelmo Gernum; et aliis.

Datum per manum nostram apud Notingham, vicesimo die Julii, anno regni nostri tricesimo nono.   4155.

VI.—*Third Charter of King Henry III.*

1272, April 14.

Henry III. third charter.

¹[H]ENRICUS, Dei gratia, Rex Angliae, Dominus Hiberniae et Dux Aquitanniae, archiepiscopis, episcopis, abbatibus, prioribus, comitibus, baronibus, justitiariis, vicecomitibus, praepositis, ministris et omnibus ballivis et fidelibus suis, salutem.

The Burgesses shall not be arrested out of the borough for any debts of which they are not principals or sureties.

Sciatis nos concessisse, et hac praesenti carta nostra confirmasse, Burgensibus nostris Notinghamm', quod ipsi, et eorum heredes, imperpetuum, per totam terram et potestatem nostram, habeant hanc libertatem, videlicet, quod ipsi, vel eorum bona quocumque locorum in potestate nostra inventa, non arestentur pro aliquo debito de quo fidejussores aut principales debitores non extiterint.

Grant of return of writs.

Concessimus etiam eisdem Burgensibus, quod imperpetuum habeant returnum brevium nostrorum de summonitionibus Scaccarii nostri de omnibus ad burgum nostrum Notingham' pertinentibus, ita quod nullus vicecomes, aut alius ballivus vel minister noster, decetero intromittat se de hujusmodi summonitionibus

---

¹ This is little more than a recital of the second charter (No. V.).

return of our writs of summons of our Exchequer, in everything Henry III. pertaining to our borough of Nottingham, so that no sheriff, or other bailiff or minister of ours, shall hereafter intermeddle with the making of such summonses or distresses in the aforesaid borough, unless through the default of the said Burgesses or Bailiffs of the same borough.

Wherefore we will and firmly enjoin, for us and our heirs, Enactment that the aforesaid Burgesses and their heirs shall have for ever clause. the before-written liberties, as is aforesaid. And we prohibit, under pain of forfeiture to us of ten pounds, any one from vexing, disturbing, or disquieting them against these liberties.

These being witnesses: Roger le Bigot, Earl of Norfolk, Marshal of England; Ralph Fitz-Nicholas; John de Lexington; Richard de Grey; William de Grey; Humbert Poieys; Walkelin de Arden; Peter Everard; William Gernon; and others.

Given by our hands at Nottingham, the twentieth day of July, in the thirty-ninth year of our reign. 4155.

VI.—*Third Charter of King Henry III.*

1272, April 14.

[1] HENRY, by the grace of God, King of England, Lord of Henry III. Ireland, and Duke of Aquitaine, to his archbishops, bishops, third charter. abbots, priors, earls, barons, justices, sheriffs, reeves, ministers and all his bailiffs and faithful subjects, greeting.

Know ye that we have granted, and by this our present The Burgesses charter have confirmed, to our Burgesses of Nottingham that arrested out they, and their heirs, shall have for ever, throughout our whole of the borough for land and jurisdiction, this liberty, to wit, that they, or their any debts of which they goods found in whatsoever place in our jurisdiction, shall not are not principals or be arrested for any debt of which they are not the pledges or sureties. principal debtors.

We have also granted to the same Burgesses that they shall Grant of return of writs. have for ever the return of our writs of summons of our Exchequer of all things relating to our borough of Nottingham, so that no sheriff, or other our bailiff or minister, shall henceforth intermeddle with making such summonses or distraints in the

18 CHARTER OF EDWARD I. [1284

HENRY III. aut districtionibus faciendis in praedicto burgo, nisi per defectum dictorum Burgensium, aut Ballivorum ejusdem burgi.

Enactment clause. Quare volumus et firmiter praecipimus, pro nobis et heredibus nostris, quod praedicti Burgenses et eorum heredes imperpetuum habeant libertates praedictas, sicut praedictum est. Et prohibemus, super forisfacturam nostram decem librarum, ne quis eos contra libertates illas in aliquo injuste vexet, disturbet, vel inquietet.

Hiis testibus: Thoma de Clare; Petro de Chaumpvent; Willelmo de Wintreshull; Willelmo Belet; Waltero de Burges; Galfrido de Percy; Johanne Carbunel; Willelmo Arnald; et aliis.

Datum per manum nostram apud Westmonasterium, quartodecimo die Aprilis, anno regni nostri quinquagesimo sexto.

4158.

VII.—*Charter of King Edward I.*

1283-4, February 12.

EDWARD I. [1] REX archiepiscopis, *et cetera*, salutem.

Restoration of liberties seized into King's hands. Cum nos, ob certas transgressiones, quas Burgenses et Communitas villae nostrae Notingham' fecerant ex fiducia libertatum suarum, eandem villam, cum omnibus libertatibus ad ipsam spectantibus, ceperimus, et per triennium et amplius detinuerimus in manu nostra; volentes eisdem Burgensibus et Communitati gratiam facere specialem, eandem villam, cum omnibus libertatibus quas Burgenses et homines ipsius villae per cartas progenitorum nostrorum, Regum Angliae, prius habuerunt, restituimus eisdem; concedendo, pro nobis et heredibus nostris, quod iidem Burgenses et Communitas omnibus eisdem libertatibus eodem modo decetero gaudeant et utantur, quo tempore captionis villae praedictae in manum nostram eis, juxta tenorem cartarum praedictarum, rationabiliter utebantur: ita quod ipsi, et

The Burgesses to render the old ferm of £52 with an increment of £8. eorum successores, reddant de eadem villa nobis et heredibus nostris singulis annis, ad Scaccarium nostrum, quinquaginta et duas libras, in forma qua prius eas inde nobis reddere consueverunt, et quod octo libras de incremento nobis et heredibus nostris inde nichilominus reddant annuatim.

[1] The original of this charter is lost. The above text is printed from the enrolment upon the Charter Rolls in the Public Record Office.

aforesaid borough, unless through the default of the said Bur- HENRY III.
gesses, or the Bailiffs of the same borough.

Wherefore we will and firmly enjoin, for us and our heirs, Enactment
that the aforesaid Burgesses and their heirs for ever shall have clause.
the aforesaid liberties, as is aforesaid. And we forbid, under
penalty of forfeiture to us of ten pounds, any one from unjustly
vexing, disturbing, or disquieting them in aught against these
liberties.

These being witnesses: Thomas de Clare; Peter de Chaumpvent; William de Wintershill; William Belet; Walter de
Burges; Geoffrey de Percy; John Carbunel; William Arnold;
and others.

Given by our hand at Westminster, the fourteenth day of
April, in the fifty-sixth year of our reign. 4158.

VII.—*Charter of King Edward I.*
1283-4, February 12.

[1] THE KING to his archbishops, *et cetera*, greeting. EDWARD I.

Whereas we, on account of certain transgressions which the Restoration of
Burgesses and Community of our town of Nottingham had liberties
committed out of confidence in their liberties, have taken the King's hands.
same town, with all liberties pertaining to it, and have detained
it in our hands for three years and more; wishing to show the
same Burgesses and Community special grace, we restore to
them the same town, with all the liberties which the Burgesses
and men of that town had before by the charters of our progenitors, Kings of England; granting, for us and our heirs, that
the same Burgesses and Community may enjoy and use all the
same liberties henceforth in the same manner as at the time of the
taking of the aforesaid town into our hands they reasonably
used them, according to the tenor of the aforesaid charters: on
condition that they, and their successors, render from the same The Burgesses
town to us and our heirs each year, at our Exchequer, fifty-two old ferm of
pounds, in the form in which they were before accustomed to £52 with an
render them to us therefor, and that they render annually £8.
therefor notwithstanding to us and our heirs eight pounds by
way of increment.

They may elect a Mayor, Et ad relevationem status Burgensium et aliorum hominum ejusdem villae, concessimus, pro nobis et heredibus nostris, quod ipsi decetero habeant in eadem villa unum Majorem de se ipsis, quem, congregatis burgensibus utriusque burgi ejusdem villae singulis annis in festo Sancti Michaëlis, unanimi consensu et voluntate eligant, ut praesit Ballivis et aliis de eadem villa in omnibus, quae[1] pertinent ad utriusque burgi ejusdem villae regimen et juvamen, et quod statim, eadem electione facta, *and one Bailiff for each of the two Boroughs of the town.* eligant unum Ballivum de uno burgo et alium de alio burgo, pro diversitate consuetudinum in eisdem burgis habitarum, qui ea, quae pertinent ad officium suum, exequantur.

Grant of a Fair at feast of St. Edmund. Et quod ipsi, et eorum successores, praeter feriam suam per octo dies ad festum Sancti Matthaei Apostoli durantem, habeant imperpetuum unam aliam feriam in eadem villa singulis annis per quindecim dies duraturam, videlicet, in vigilia, in die, et in crastino festi Sancti Edmundi Regis et Martiris, et per duodecim dies sequentes, nisi feria illa sit ad nocumentum vicinarum feriarum.

Nov. 20.

Enactment clause. Quare volumus et firmiter praecipimus, pro nobis et heredibus nostris, quod praedicti Burgenses et homines, et eorum successores, praeter feriam suam per octo dies ad festum Sancti Matthaei Apostoli durantem, habeant imperpetuum unam aliam feriam in eadem villa singulis annis per quindecim dies duraturam, videlicet, in vigilia, in die, et in crastino festi Sancti Edmundi Regis et Martiris, et per duodecim dies sequentes, cum omnibus libertatibus et liberis consuetudinibus ad hujusmodi feriam pertinentibus, nisi feria illa sit ad nocumentum vicinarum feriarum, sicut praedictum est.

Hiis testibus: venerabilibus patribus R[oberto], Bathoniensi et Wellensi, et A[ntonio], Dunolmensi, Episcopis; Thoma de Clare; Ottone de Grandisono; Johanne de Vescy; Roberto Tibetot; Roberto, filio Johannis; et aliis.

Datum *ut supra* [*i.e.,* 'Datum per manum nostram apud Lincoln, xij. die Februarii'].

Rot. Chartarum, 12 Ed. I., No. 51.

---

[1] *quae,*] 'qui,' MS.

And we have granted, for us and our heirs, for the alleviation of the estate of the Burgesses and other men of the same town, that they shall henceforth have in the same town a Mayor from amongst themselves, whom, the burgesses of both boroughs of the same town being assembled each year in the feast of Saint Michael, they shall elect with unanimous consent and will, to be set over the Bailiffs and others of the same borough in everything pertaining to the government and advantage of both boroughs of the same town, and that they shall at once, the same election having been made, elect one Bailiff of one borough and another for the other borough, on account of the diversity of customs existing in the same boroughs, who shall execute those things which pertain to their office. *They may elect a Mayor, and one Bailiff for each of the two boroughs of the town.*

And that they, and their successors, besides their fair lasting for eight days at the feast of Saint Matthew the Apostle, shall have for ever one other fair in the same town each year to endure for fifteen days, that is to say, on the eve, the day, and the morrow of the feast of Saint Edmund the King and Martyr, and for the twelve days following, unless this fair shall be to the damage of neighbouring fairs. *Grant of a Fair at feast of St. Edmund. Nov. 20.*

Wherefore we will and firmly enjoin, for ourselves and our heirs, that the aforesaid Burgesses and men and their successors, besides their fair lasting for eight days at the feast of Saint Matthew the Apostle, shall have for ever one other fair in the same town every year to endure for fifteen days, to wit, on the eve, the day, and the morrow of the feast of Saint Edmund the King and Martyr, and for the twelve days following, with all liberties and free customs pertaining to such a fair, unless this fair shall be to the damage of neighbouring fairs, as is aforesaid. *Enactment clause.*

These being witnesses: the venerable fathers Robert, Bishop of Bath and Wells, and Antony, Bishop of Durham; Thomas de Clare; Otto de Grandison; John de Vescy; Robert Tibetot; Robert Fitz-John; and others.

Given *as above* [*i.e.*, 'Given by our hand at Lincoln, on the 12th day of February'].

Rot. Chartarum, 12 Ed. I., No. 51.

VIII.—*Charter of King Edward II.*
1313-14, March 16.

Edward II. [E]DWARDUS, Dei gratia, Rex Angliae, Dominus Hiberniae, et Dux Aquitanniae, archiepiscopis, episcopis, abbatibus, prioribus, comitibus, baronibus, justitiariis, vicecomitibus, praepositis, ministris, et omnibus ballivis et fidelibus suis, salutem.

Recital of previous charters. Inspeximus cartam confirmationis, quam Dominus Henricus, quondam Rex Angliae, avus noster, fecit Burgensibus de Notingham in haec verba: 'HENRICUS, Dei gratia' [*etc., reciting the first charter of Henry III., No. IV.*]. Inspeximus etiam quandam aliam cartam quam idem avus noster fecit eisdem Burgensibus, in haec verba: 'HENRICUS, Dei gratia' [*etc., reciting second charter of Henry III., No. V.*]. Inspeximus insuper cartam quam celebris memoriae Dominus Edwardus, quondam Rex Angliae, pater noster, fecit eisdem Burgensibus in haec verba: 'EDWARDUS, Dei gratia' [*etc., reciting the charter of Edward I., No. VII.*].

Confirmation of same. Nos autem, concessiones, confirmationes et restitutionem praedictas ratas habentes et gratas, eas pro nobis et heredibus nostris, quantum in nobis est, praefatis Burgensibus et eorum heredibus ac successoribus, Burgensibus ejusdem villae, concedimus et confirmamus, sicut cartae praedictae rationabiliter testantur.

The Burgesses shall not lose their rights through non-user. Et insuper concessimus eis, pro nobis et heredibus nostris, quod, licet ipsi vel eorum antecessores, Burgenses ejusdem villae, aliqua vel aliquibus libertatum praedictarum hactenus usi non fuerint, ipsi tamen et heredes ac successores sui libertatibus illis, et earum qualibet, sine occasione vel impedimento nostri, vel heredum nostrorum, justitiariorum, escaëtorum, vicecomitum, aut aliorum ballivorum seu ministrorum nostrorum quorumcunque, decetero plene gaudeant et utantur.

They shall not plead out of the Borough concerning lands, etc., in the same, Praeterea, volentes eisdem Burgensibus gratiam facere ampliorem, concessimus eis, pro nobis et heredibus nostris, ad meliorationem praedictae villae nostrae Notingham', et commoditatem Burgensium nostrorum ejusdem villae, ut eo tranquillius negotiationibus suis intendere possint, quod nullus eorum placitet aut implacitetur coram nobis, vel heredibus nostris, aut aliquibus justitiariis nostris, vel heredum nostrorum, extra burgum prae-

VIII.—*Charter of King Edward II.*
1313-14, March 16.

EDWARD, by the grace of God, King of England, Lord of Ireland, and Duke of Aquitaine, to his archbishops, bishops, abbots, priors, earls, barons, justices, sheriffs, reeves, ministers, and all his bailiffs and faithful subjects, greeting. *[margin: Edward II.]*

We have inspected the charter of confirmation which Lord Henry, sometime King of England, our grandfather, made to the Burgesses of Nottingham in these words: 'HENRY, by the grace of God' [*etc., reciting the first charter of Henry III., No. IV.*]. We have also inspected a certain other charter which the same our grandfather made to the same Burgesses in these words: 'HENRY, by the grace of God' [*etc., reciting second charter of Henry III., No. V.*]. We have also inspected the charter which the Lord Edward of famous memory, sometime King of England, our father, made to the same Burgesses in these words: 'EDWARD, by the grace of God' [*etc., reciting the charter of Edward I., No. VII.*]. *[margin: Recital of previous charters.]*

We, esteeming the aforesaid grants, confirmations and restitution as valid and acceptable, do grant and confirm them for us and our heirs, so far as in us lies, to the aforesaid Burgesses and their heirs, and successors, Burgesses of the same town, as the charters aforesaid do reasonably witness. *[margin: Confirmation of same.]*

And moreover, we have granted to them, for ourselves and our heirs, that, although they or their ancestors, Burgesses of the same town, may not have used up to this time any of the aforesaid liberties, they and their heirs and successors may yet henceforth fully enjoy and use those liberties, and each of them, without impediment or hindrance from us, or our heirs, or from our justices, escheators, sheriffs, or others our bailiffs or ministers whatsoever. *[margin: The Burgesses shall not lose their rights through non-user.]*

Moreover, desiring to shew more ample grace to the same Burgesses, we have granted to them, for us and our heirs, for the amelioration of our said town of Nottingham, and for the advantage of our Burgesses of the same town, so that they may the more tranquilly attend to their affairs, that none of them shall plead or be impleaded before us, or our heirs, or any justices of us, or our heirs, without the aforesaid borough, as to *[margin: They shall not plead out of the Borough concerning lands, etc., in the same,]*

CHARTER OF EDWARD II. [1314

EDWARD II.

unless the actions concern the Crown or the Community of the Borough.

dictum, de terris aut tenementis, quae sunt in burgo praedicto, seu de transgressionibus aut contractibus, vel aliis quibuscumque, in eodem burgo factis vel emergentibus, set omnia hujusmodi placita, quae coram nobis, vel heredibus nostris, aut aliquibus justitiariis nostris de Banco, vel aliis, summoneri contigerit vel attachiari extra burgum praedictum placitanda, coram Majore et Ballivis burgi praedicti, qui pro tempore fuerint, infra burgum praedictum placitentur et terminentur, nisi placita illa tangant nos vel heredes nostros, seu Communitatem burgi praedicti. Et

They shall not be joined with foreigners in assizes, juries, etc.

quod non ponantur cum hominibus forinsecis in assisis, juratis, aut inquisitionibus aliquibus, quae ratione tenementi, vel transgressionum, aut aliorum negotiorum forinsecorum quorumcumque, coram justitiariis aut aliis ministris nostris, vel heredum nostrorum, emersint faciendae. Nec quod homines forinseci

Foreigners shall not be joined with them in assizes, juries, etc., concerning lands or suits in the Borough.

ponantur cum ipsis Burgensibus in assisis, juratis, aut inquisitionibus aliquibus, quae ratione terrae vel tenementi in eodem burgo existentium, aut transgressionum, contractuum, seu aliorum negotiorum intrinsecorum, in eodem burgo emersint capiendae; set assisae illae, juratae, et inquisitiones de hiis quae in dicto burgo fuerint emergentes, per Burgenses ejusdem villae, et in eodem burgo solummodo, fiant, nisi res ipsae tangant nos, vel heredes nostros, seu Communitatem ejusdem burgi.

No royal officer shall enter the Borough to execute writs, etc., except in default of the Burgesses.

Et insuper, cum Burgenses illi, per cartas praedictas, habeant returna brevium nostrorum et summonitionum de Scaccario nostro de omnibus dictum burgum contingentibus, et quidam ministri nostri, et progenitorum nostrorum praedictorum, nichilominus burgum praedictum hactenus pluries sint ingressi ad districtiones et attachiamenta ibidem facienda, quae per Ballivos ejusdem villae fieri deberent: concessimus eis, pro nobis et heredibus nostris, quod nullus vicecomes, ballivus, aut alii ministri nostri, vel heredum nostrorum, quicumque dictum burgum ingrediantur ad summonitiones, attachiamenta, seu districtiones, aut alia officia ibidem facienda, nisi in defectum Ballivorum ejusdem villae qui pro tempore erunt.

Grant of immunity from various imposts.

Concedimus etiam eisdem Burgensibus, pro nobis et heredibus nostris, quod ipsi, et eorum heredes ac successores praedicti, de muragio, pavagio, stallagio, terragio, kaiagio, lastagio et passagio, per totum regnum nostrum et totam potestatem nostram, imperpetuum sint quieti.

lands or tenements which are in the borough aforesaid, or of transgressions or contracts, or other things whatsoever, done or arising in the same borough, but all such pleas which it may happen shall be summoned or attached to be pleaded out of the aforesaid borough in the presence of us, or our heirs, or any of our justices of Bench, or others, shall be pleaded and determined within the said borough before the Mayor and Bailiffs of the aforesaid borough for the time being, unless the pleas touch us or our heirs, or the Community of the aforesaid borough. And that they shall not be placed with men from outside in any assizes, juries, or inquests which may chance to be made before our justices or other ministers of us, or our heirs, by reason of tenements or trespasses, or other extraneous matters whatsoever. Nor shall men from outside be placed with the Burgesses in any assizes, juries, or inquests, which may chance to be taken in the same borough touching lands or tenements lying in the same borough, or trespasses, contracts, or other intrinsic matters; but that assizes, juries, and inquests of those things which may be arising in the said borough, shall only be made by the Burgesses of the same town, and in the same borough, unless the affairs touch us, or our heirs, or the Community of the same borough. *[EDWARD II. — unless the actions concern the Crown or the Community of the Borough. They shall not be joined with foreigners in assizes, juries, etc. Foreigners shall not be joined with them in assizes, juries, etc., concerning lands or suits in the Borough.]*

And moreover, since the Burgesses should have, by the aforesaid charters, the return of our writs and summons of our Exchequer of all things touching the said borough, and certain ministers of ours, and of our aforesaid progenitors, have notwithstanding up to this time many times entered the same borough to make distresses and attachments there, which ought to have been made by the Bailiffs of the same town: we have granted to them, for us and our heirs, that no sheriff, bailiff, or other ministers whatsoever of ours, or our heirs, shall enter the said borough to make summons, attachments, or distresses, or other duties there, unless by default of the Bailiffs of the same town for the time being. *[No royal officer shall enter the Borough to execute writs, etc., except in default of the Burgesses.]*

We also grant to the same Burgesses, for us and our heirs, that they, and their heirs and successors aforesaid, shall be quit of murage, pavage, stallage, terrage, quayage, lastage, and passage, throughout our whole kingdom and our whole dominion, for ever. *[Grant of immunity from various imposts.]*

EDWARD II.

Hiis testibus : venerabilibus patribus Waltero, Archiepiscopo Cantuariensi totius Angliae Primate, et Waltero, Coventrensi et Lych[feldensi], Episcopo ; Adomaro de Valentia, Comite Pembrochiae ; Humfrido de Bohun, Comite Herefordiae et Essexiae; Hugone le Despencer; Willelmo le Latymer; Theobaldo de Verdon ; Johanne de Crumbwell'; Edmundo de Malo Lacu, Senescallo Hospitii nostri ; et aliis.

Datum per manum nostram apud Westmonasterium, sextodecimo die Martii, anno regni nostri septimo. W. Sutton.

Per finem ducentarum marcarum.

4160.

IX.—*Charter of King Edward III.*
1330, May 1.

EDWARD III.

[E]DWARDUS, Dei gratia, Rex Angliae, Dominus Hiberniae, et Dux Aquitanniae, archiepiscopis, episcopis, abbatibus, prioribus, comitibus, baronibus, justitiariis, vicecomitibus, praepositis, ministris, et omnibus ballivis et fidelibus suis, salutem.

Confirmation of previous charters.

Inspeximus cartam celebris memoriae Domini Edwardi nuper Regis Angliae, patris nostri, in haec verba : 'EDWARDUS, Dei gratia' [*etc., reciting Edward II.'s Charter, No. VIII.*].

Nos autem, concessiones, confirmationes et restitutionem praedictas ratas habentes et gratas, eas, pro nobis et heredibus nostris, quantum in nobis est, praefatis Burgensibus, et eorum heredibus ac successoribus, Burgensibus ejusdem villae, concedimus et confirmamus, sicut cartae praedictae plenius testantur.

Restoration of the borough to the Burgesses.

Praeterea, cum dicta villa Notingham', una cum libertatibus ejusdem, in instanti itinere dilectorum et fidelium nostrorum Willelmi de Herle, et sociorum suorum, Justitiariorum nostrorum Itinerantium in Comitatu Notingham', quibusdam certis de causis, per considerationem ejusdem Curiae, capta sit in manum nostram :[1] nos, volentes eisdem Majori et Burgensibus gratiam in hac parte facere specialem, restituimus eis villam praedictam, cum omnibus libertatibus praedictis : habendam et tenendam sibi, heredibus et successoribus suis Burgensibus ejusdem villae, imperpetuum, adeo plene et integre sicut eam per

---

[1] The proceedings in *Quo Warranto* in 1329, which ended in the seizure of liberties here referred to, are printed in the *Borough Records*, vol. iii., p. 202 *sqq.*

These being witnesses: the venerable fathers Walter, Arch- *Edward II.*
bishop of Canterbury, Primate of all England, and Walter,
Bishop of Coventry and Lichfield; Aymar de Valence, Earl of
Pembroke; Humphrey de Bohun, Earl of Hereford and Essex;
Hugh le Despencer; William le Latymer; Theobald de
Verdun; John de Cromwell; Edmund de Mauley, Steward of
our Household; and others.

Given by our hands at Westminster, on the sixteenth day of
March, in the seventh year of our reign.   W. Sutton.
By a fine of two hundred marks.
4160.

IX.—*Charter of King Edward III.*

1330, May 1.

EDWARD, by the grace of God, King of England, Lord of *Edward III.*
Ireland, and Duke of Aquitaine, to his archbishops, bishops,
abbots, priors, earls, barons, justices, sheriffs, reeves, ministers,
and all his bailiffs and faithful subjects, greeting.

We have inspected the charter of Lord Edward of renowned *Confirmation of previous charters.*
memory, sometime King of England, our father, in these words:
'EDWARD, by the grace of God' [*etc., reciting Edward II.'s Charter, No. VIII.*].

We, regarding the concessions, confirmations and restitution
aforesaid as firm and acceptable, do grant and confirm them, for
us and our heirs, so far as in us lies, to the aforesaid Burgesses,
and their heirs and successors, Burgesses of the same town, as the
aforesaid charters more fully witness.

Moreover, since the said town of Nottingham, together with *Restoration of the borough to the Burgesses.*
the liberties of the same, in the present eyre of our well-beloved
and faithful William de Herle and his associates, our Justices
Itinerant in the County of Nottingham, on account of certain
specific causes, by the judgment of the same Court, has been
taken into our hands:[1] we, wishing to show to the same Mayor
and Burgesses special grace in this particular, do restore to
them the town aforesaid, with all the aforesaid liberties: to have
and to hold to them, and their heirs for ever, Burgesses of the

cartas praedictas tenuerunt et tenere debuerunt ante captionem supradictam.

Reinforcement of the grant of return of writs.

Insuper, cum in carta praedicti Henrici Regis, proavi nostri, contineatur, quod praedicti Burgenses, et eorum heredes imperpetuum, haberent returnum brevium ipsius proavi nostri et heredum suorum de summonitione Scaccarii sui, de omnibus ad dictum burgum Notingham' spectantibus, et quod nullus vicecomes aut alius ballivus ipsius proavi nostri, vel heredum suorum, quicumque dictum burgum ingrederentur ad summonitiones, attachiamenta, seu districtiones, aut alia officia ibidem facienda, nisi in defectum Ballivorum ejusdem villae;[1] et praedicti Burgenses et antecessores sui, eo praetextu, hucusque habuerunt returna omnium brevium progenitorum nostrorum, et nostrorum, tam de summonitionibus Scaccarii, quam aliorum brevium quorumcumque, eundum burgum qualitercumque tangentium : Nos, securitati eorumdem Burgensium, ne super hoc inquietari possint infuturum, providere volentes, concessimus eis, et hac carta nostra confirmavimus, quod ipsi, et eorum heredes et successores praedicti imperpetuum, habeant returna omnium brevium nostrorum, et heredum nostrorum, tam de summonitionibus Scaccarii, quam aliorum brevium quorumcumque, praedictum burgum qualitercumque tangentium ; ita quod nullus vicecomes, ballivus, seu alius minister noster, vel heredum nostrorum, burgum illum ingrediatur ad summonitiones, attachiamenta, seu districtiones, vel aliqua alia officia, infra eundem burgum, exercenda vel facienda, nisi in defectum Ballivorum villae supradictae, sicut praedictum est.

Confirmation of the right to have a gaol.

Ad haec, cum per quandam inquisitionem, per praefatum Willelmum et dilectum et fidelem nostrum Nicholaum Fastolft de mandato nostro factam, et in Cancellaria[m] nostra[m] retornatam, compertum sit, quod praedicti Burgenses, a tempore quo non extat memoria usque ad tempus confectionis dictae cartae praedicti Johannis Regis, progenitoris nostri, eisdem Burgensibus factae, et etiam postmodum, gaolam in dicta villa Notingham' habuerunt, pro custodia eorum qui in eadem villa capti fuerunt seu attachiati, et quod gaola illa fuit in custodia eorum, qui custodiam villae praedictae habuerunt, tanquam ad eandem

---

[1] Cf. Charter of Henry III., No. V.

same town, as fully and wholly as they held it, and should have held it, by the aforesaid charters before the aforesaid seizure.

Edward III.

Moreover, whereas it is contained in the charter of the aforesaid King Henry, our great-grandfather, that the aforesaid Burgesses, and their heirs should have for ever, the return of the writs of the same our great-grandfather, and his heirs, of summons of his Exchequer, of all things belonging to the said borough of Nottingham, and that no sheriff or other bailiff whatsoever of our same great-grandfather, or of his heirs, should enter the said borough to make summonses, attachments or distresses, or other offices there, except through the default of the Bailiffs of the same town;[1] and the aforesaid Burgesses and their ancestors, on that account, have had up to this time the return of all writs of our progenitors, and of ours, as well of summons of the Exchequer, as of other writs whatsoever, touching the same borough in any way soever: We, wishing to provide for the security of the same Burgesses that they may not herein in the future be disquieted, have granted them, and by this our charter have confirmed, that they, and their heirs and successors aforesaid for ever, shall have the return of all writs of ours, and of our heirs, as well of summonses of the Exchequer as of other writs whatsoever, in any wise whatsoever relating to the said borough; so that no sheriff, bailiff or other minister of ours, or of our heirs, shall enter that borough to make or perform summonses, attachments, or distresses, or any other offices, within the same borough, except through the default of the Bailiffs of the abovesaid town, as is aforesaid.

Reinforcement of the grant of return of writs.

Moreover, whereas it appears by a certain inquisition made, by the aforesaid William and our well-beloved and faithful Nicholas Fastolf, at our command, and returned into our Chancery, that the aforesaid Burgesses, from time whereof memory does not exist until the time of the making of the said charter of the aforesaid King John, our progenitor, made to the said Burgesses, and also afterwards, have had a gaol in the said town of Nottingham, for the custody of those who were taken or attached in the same town, and that that gaol was in the custody of those who had charge of the town aforesaid, as pertaining to the same town, as well whilst that town was in the hands of our progenitors aforesaid, as when it was in the hands

Confirmation of the right to have a gaol.

EDWARD III. villam pertinens, tam dum villa illa fuit in manibus progenitorum nostrorum praedictorum, quam in manibus Burgensium villae supradictae: Nos, pro pleniori securitate ipsorum, volentes eis gratiam in hac parte facere specialem, concessimus eis, et hac carta nostra confirmavimus, quod iidem Burgenses, heredes et successores sui praedicti imperpetuum, habeant gaolam praedictam in villa praedicta, pro custodia illorum qui in eadem villa, ex quacumque causa, capi seu attachiari contigeri[n]t.

Confirmation of the Saturday Market.   Insuper, cum praefati Burgenses, praetextu dictorum verborum in praedictis chartis contentorum quod 'homines de Notinghamshire et de Derbishire venire debent ad praedictum burgum de Notingham die Veneris et Sabbati cum quadrigis et summagiis suis,'[1] habuerint in eodem burgo unum mercatum singulis septimanis per diem Sabbati, sicut dicunt: Nos, ne praedicti Burgenses super dicto mercato suo occasionentur infuturum, volentes eorum securitati prospicere gratiose, concessimus eis, et hac carta nostra confirmavimus, quod ipsi, et heredes ac successores sui praedicti imperpetuum, habeant et teneant mercatum praedictum singulis septimanis per diem Sabbati, cum omnibus libertatibus et liberis consuetudinibus ad hujusmodi mercatum pertinentibus; nolentes quod ipsi, vel eorum heredes vel successores, occasione mercati illius, pro tempore praeterito vel futuro, per nos, vel heredes nostros, seu ministros nostros quoscumque occasionentur, molestentur in aliquo, seu graventur.

Acquittance of pontage.   Concessimus etiam eisdem Burgensibus, et hac carta nostra confirmavimus, quod ipsi, heredes et successores sui, de pontagio per totum regnum et potestatem nostram imperpetuum sint quieti.

Enactment clause.   Quare volumus et firmiter praecipimus, pro nobis et heredibus nostris, quod iidem Burgenses, et eorum heredes ac successores, imperpetuum habeant et teneant praedictam villam, cum omnibus libertatibus praedictis; et etiam imperpetuum habeant returna omnium brevium nostrorum et heredum nostrorum, tam de summonitionibus Scaccarii, quam aliorum brevium quorumcumque; et etiam gaolam in eadem villa; et mercatum per dictum diem Sabbati, cum omnibus libertatibus et liberis consuetudinibus ad hujusmodi mercatum pertinentibus; quodque quieti sint de hujusmodi pontagio per totum regnum et potestatem nostram, sicut praedictum est.

of the Burgesses of the town aforesaid: We, desiring in this par- Edward III.
ticular to show them special grace, for their more ample security,
have granted them, and by this our charter have confirmed, that
the same Burgesses, their heirs and successors aforesaid for ever,
shall have the aforesaid gaol in the aforesaid town, for the
custody of those who shall happen to be taken or attached in
the same town, from whatsoever cause.

Moreover, whereas the aforesaid Burgesses, by reason of the Confirmation of the Saturday Market.
said words contained in the aforesaid charters that 'the men of
Nottinghamshire and of Derbyshire should come to the aforesaid borough of Nottingham on Friday and Saturday with their
wains and pack-horses,'[1] have had in the same borough a
market every week during Saturday, as they say: We, desiring
graciously to provide for their security, so that the aforesaid
Burgesses may not in future be molested as to the said market,
have granted them, and by this our present charter have confirmed, that they, and their heirs and successors aforesaid for
ever, may have and hold the aforesaid market each week during
Saturday, with all liberties and free customs pertaining to such
market; we being unwilling that they, or their heirs or successors,
on account of that market should be impeded, molested or in
any wise troubled by us, or our heirs, or our ministers whatsoever, for time past or to come.

We have also granted to the same Burgesses, and by this Acquittance of pontage.
our present charter have confirmed, that they, their heirs and
successors, shall be for ever quit of pontage throughout our
whole kingdom and dominion.

Wherefore we will and firmly enjoin, for us and our heirs, Enactment clause.
that the same Burgesses, and their heirs and successors, shall
have and hold for ever the aforesaid town, with all the aforesaid
liberties; and also shall have for ever the return of all writs of
ours and of our heirs, as well of summonses of the Exchequer,
as of other writs whatsoever; and also a gaol in the same town;
and a market for the said Saturday, with all liberties and free
customs pertaining to such market; and that they shall be quit
of such pontage throughout our whole kingdom and dominion,
as is aforesaid.

---

[1] Cf. Charter of Henry II., No. I.

Hiis testibus: venerabilibus patribus Henrico, Episcopo Lincolniensi, Cancellario nostro; Johanne, Wyntoniensi, et Rogero, Coventrensi et Lichefeldensi, Episcopis; Johanne de Eltham, Comite Cornubiae, fratre nostro carissimo; Rogero de Mortuo Mari, Comite Marchiae; Willelmo de Monte Acuto; Johanne Mautravers, Senescallo Hospitii nostri; et aliis.

Datum per manum nostram, apud Wodestok, primo die Maii, anno regni nostri quarto.

Per ipsum Regem et Concilium.

4161.

X.—*Letters Patent regarding the election of the Bailiffs.*

1330, May 3.

EDWARDUS, Dei gratia, Rex Angliae, Dominus Hiberniae et Dux Aquitanniae, omnibus ad quos praesentes litterae pervenerint, salutem.

Sciatis, quod, cum per cartam celebris memoriae Domini Edwardi, nuper Regis Angliae, avi nostri, concessum existat Burgensibus villae nostrae Notingham', quod iidem Burgenses, singulis annis, in festo Sancti Michaëlis, eligant unum Majorem de se ipsis, 'ut praesit Ballivis et aliis de eadem villa in omnibus quae pertinent ad utriusque burgi villae illius regimen et juvamen, et quod statim, eadem electione facta, eligant unum Ballivum de uno burgo et alium de alio burgo, pro diversitate consuetudinum in eisdem burgis habitarum, qui ea, quae pertinent ad officium suum, exequantur;'[1] et praefati Burgenses nobis supplicaverint quod, cum ipsi in uno burgorum praedictorum, propter paupertatem et insufficientiam inhabitantium in eodem, ballivum sufficientem ad officium illud exequendum ad praesens nequeant invenire, velimus eis concedere, quod ipsi in eadem villa, in locis ubi melius viderint expedire, dictos duos ballivos eligere possint: Nos, eorum supplicationi favorabiliter annuentes in hac parte, concessimus eis quod ipsi, post electionem de eodem Majore, ut praemittitur, factam, dictos duos Ballivos de melioribus et magis sufficientibus ejusdem villae, in locis ubi melius viderint expedire, qui ea, quae ad officium suum pertinent

---

[1] Cf. Charter of Edward I., No. VII.

These being witnesses: the venerable fathers Henry, Bishop of Lincoln, our Chancellor; John, Bishop of Winchester, and Roger, Bishop of Coventry and Lichfield; John de Eltham, Earl of Cornwall, our dearest brother; Roger de Mortimer, Earl of March; William de Montacute; John Maltravers, Steward of our Household; and others.

Given by our hand at Woodstock, the first day of May, in the fourth year of our reign.   By the King and Council.

4161.

X.—*Letters Patent regarding the election of the Bailiffs.*

1330, May 3.

EDWARD, by the grace of God, King of England, Lord of Ireland and Duke of Aquitaine, to all to whom the present letters shall come, greeting.

Know ye that, whereas by the charter of Lord Edward of renowned memory, late King of England, our grandfather, it was granted to the Burgesses of our town of Nottingham that the same Burgesses, in each year, in the feast of Saint Michael, should elect a Mayor from themselves 'to be set over the Bailiffs and others of the same borough in everything that pertains to the government and advantage of the same town, and that they shall at once, the same election having been made, elect one Bailiff of one borough and another for the other borough, on account of the diversity of customs existing in the same boroughs, who shall execute those things that pertain to their office;[1] and the aforesaid Burgesses have besought us that, whereas in one of the boroughs aforesaid, on account of the poverty and insufficiency of the inhabitants of the same, they are unable at present to find a sufficient bailiff to execute that office, we should grant them that in the same town, in places which may seem to be most expedient, they may elect the said two bailiffs: We, favourably inclining to their prayer in this particular, have granted them that they, after the election of the same Mayor has been made, as is aforesaid, shall have power to elect the said two Bailiffs out of the better and more sufficient persons of the same town, in places which may seem to them to be most expedient, who shall execute those things that

EDWARD III. exequantur, eligere valeant, dictis verbis in praedicta carta ipsius avi nostri contentis non obstantibus.

In cujus rei testimonium has litteras nostras fieri fecimus patentes, quamdiu nobis placuerit duraturas. Teste me ipso apud Wodestok, primo die Maii, anno regni nostri quarto.

Per ipsum Regem et Concilium.

4312.

XI.—*Grant of a Fair to the Burgesses in place of the Fair at the Feast of St. Edmund.*

1377-8, March 19.

RICHARD II. RICARDUS, Dei gratia, Rex Angliae et Franciae, et Dominus Hiberniae, archiepiscopis, episcopis, abbatibus, prioribus, ducibus, comitibus, baronibus, justitiariis, vicecomitibus, praepositis, ballivis, ministris, et aliis fidelibus suis, salutem.

Grant of a fair at the feast of St. Peter in place of that at the feast of St. Edmund.

Sept. 21.

Nov. 20.

Feb. 22.

Supplicaverunt nobis dilecti nobis Major, Ballivi, et Burgenses villae nostrae de Notyngham, ut, cum ipsi, per cartas progenitorum nostrorum, quondam Regum Angliae, habeant singulis annis, in villa praedicta, duas ferias, unam, videlicet, per octo dies ad festum Sancti Mathaei Apostoli durantem, et alteram per quindecim dies, videlicet, in vigilia, in die et in crastino Sancti Edmundi Regis et Martiris, et per duodecim dies sequentes, velimus eis gratiose concedere ut ipsi, loco secundae feriae praedictae, habeant unam feriam ibidem per quinque dies duraturam, videlicet, in die et in crastino Sancti Petri in Cathedra, et per tres dies proxime sequentes: nos, eorum supplicationi in hac parte annuentes, de gratia nostra speciali concessimus, pro nobis et heredibus nostris, praefatis Majori, Ballivis, et Burgensibus, quod ipsi et eorum successores imperpetuum, praeter primam feriam suam praedictam, habeant, loco secundae feriae quindecim dierum, unam feriam apud villam praedictam singulis annis per quinque dies duraturam, videlicet, in die et in crastino Sancti Petri in Cathedra, et per tres dies proxime sequentes, sicut praedictum est; dum tamen feria illa non sit ad nocumentum vicinarum feriarum.

Recapitulation. Quare volumus et firmiter praecipimus, pro nobis et heredibus nostris, quod praedicti Major, Ballivi, et Burgenses, et eorum successores imperpetuum, praeter primam feriam suam praedictam, habeant, loco suae secundae feriae praedictae

pertain to their office, the said words contained in the aforesaid EDWARD III. charter of our grandfather notwithstanding.

In testimony whereof we have caused these our letters to be made patent, to endure as long as it shall please us. Witness myself at Woodstock, the first day of May, in the fourth year of our reign. By the King himself and Council.

4312.

XI.—*Grant of a Fair to the Burgesses in place of the Fair at the Feast of St. Edmund.*

1377-8, March 19.

RICHARD, by the grace of God, King of England and RICHARD II. France, and Lord of Ireland, to his archbishops, bishops, abbots, priors, dukes, earls, barons, justices, sheriffs, reeves, bailiffs, ministers, and others his faithful subjects, greeting.

Our well-beloved the Mayor, Bailiffs, and Burgesses of our Grant of a fair town of Nottingham have besought us that, whereas by the St. Peter in charters of our progenitors, sometime Kings of England, they place of that have each year, in the aforesaid town, two fairs, one, to wit, St. Edmund. enduring for eight days at the feast of Saint Matthew the Sept. 21. Apostle, and the other for fifteen days, to wit, on the eve, the day and the morrow of Saint Edmund the King and Martyr, Nov. 20. and for twelve days following, we should graciously grant that they, in the place of the second fair aforesaid, should have a fair there enduring for five days, to wit, on the day and Feb. 22. the morrow of Saint Peter in Cathedra, and for three days next following: we, acceding to their supplication in this particular, have granted of our special grace, for us and our heirs, to the aforesaid Mayor, Bailiffs, and Burgesses, that they and their successors for ever, besides their first fair aforesaid, shall have, instead of the second fair of fifteen days, a fair at the aforesaid town each year to endure for five days, to wit, on the day and the morrow of Saint Peter in Cathedra, and for three days next following, as is aforesaid; provided that this fair shall not be to the damage of neighbouring fairs.

Wherefore we will and firmly enjoin, for us and our heirs, Recapitulation. that the aforesaid Mayor, Bailiffs, and Burgesses, and their successors for ever, besides their first fair aforesaid, shall have, instead of their second fair aforesaid of fifteen days, a fair at the

RICHARD II. quindecim dierum, unam feriam apud villam praedictam singulis annis per quinque dies duraturam, videlicet, in die et in crastino Sancti Petri in Cathedra, et per tres dies proxime sequentes, cum omnibus libertatibus et liberis consuetudinibus ad hujusmodi feriam pertinentibus, nisi feria illa sit ad nocumentum vicinarum feriarum, sicut praedictum est.

Hiis testibus: venerabilibus patribus Adam de Houton, Menevensi, Cancellario nostro, Thoma de Brantyngham, Exoniensi, Thesaurario nostro, Thoma, Karliolensi, Radulpho, Saresburiensi, Episcopis; Thoma de Wodestok, Buk[ingham'], Thoma de Bello Campo, Warr[wick'], Comitibus; Willelmo Latymer, Ricardo de Stafford, Henrico le Scrop, Johanne Knyvet, militibus; Ricardo le Scrop, Senescallo Hospitii nostri; et aliis.

Datum per manum nostram apud Westmonasterium, decimo nono die Martii, anno regni nostri primo. Scarle.

Per Breve de Privato Sigillo. 4165.

XII.—*Charter of King Richard II.*
1378, April 8.

RICHARD II. RICARDUS, Dei gratia, Rex Angliae et Franciae, et Dominus Hiberniae, omnibus, ad quos praesentes litterae pervenerint, salutem.

Recital of previous charters
Inspeximus cartam Domini Edwardi nuper Regis Angliae, avi nostri, in haec verba: 'EDWARDUS, Dei gratia' [*etc., reciting charter of Edward III., No. IX.*].

Confirmation of same.
Nos autem, omnes et singulas concessiones, confirmationes et restitutiones praedictas ratas habentes et gratas, eas, pro nobis et heredibus nostris, quantum in nobis est, praefatis Burgensibus villae de Notyngham, heredibus et successoribus suis, Burgensibus ejusdem villae, concedimus et confirmamus, sicut cartae praedictae rationabiliter testantur, et prout iidem Burgenses et antecessores sui libertatibus et quietantiis praedictis rationabiliter usi sunt et gavisi.

In cujus rei testimonium has litteras nostras fieri fecimus patentes. Teste me ipso apud Westmonasterium, octavo die Aprilis, anno regni nostri primo. Scarle.

Per ipsum Regem et Concilium in Parliamento, quia onerati sunt cum hominibus Derb[iae] de quadam balingera facienda.

4164.

aforesaid town each year to endure for five days, to wit, on the day and the morrow of Saint Peter in Cathedra, and for three days next following, with all liberties and free customs pertaining to such fair, unless this fair shall be to the damage of neighbouring fairs, as is aforesaid.

These being witnesses: the venerable fathers Adam de Houghton, Bishop of Saint David's, our Chancellor; Thomas de Brantingham, Bishop of Exeter, our Treasurer; Thomas, Bishop of Carlisle; Ralph, Bishop of Salisbury; Thomas de Woodstock, Earl of Buckingham; Thomas de Beauchamp, Earl of Warwick; William Latimer, Richard de Stafford, Henry le Scrope; John Knyvet, knights; Richard le Scrope, Steward of our Household; and others.

Given by our hand at Westminster, on the nineteenth day of March, in the first year of our reign. Scarle.

By Writ of Privy Seal. 4165.

XII.—*Charter of King Richard II.*

1378, April 8.

RICHARD, by the grace of God, King of England and France, and Lord of Ireland, to all to whom the present letters may come, greeting.

We have inspected the charter of the Lord Edward late King of England, our grandfather, in these words: 'EDWARD, by the grace of God' [*etc., reciting charter of Edward III., No. IX.*].

We, esteeming all and singular the aforesaid grants, confirmations and restitutions as valid and acceptable, grant and confirm them, for us and our heirs, so far as in us lies, to the aforesaid Burgesses of the town of Nottingham, their heirs and successors, Burgesses of the same town, as the charters aforesaid reasonably witness, and as the same Burgesses and their ancestors have reasonably used and enjoyed the liberties and acquittances aforesaid.

In testimony whereof we have caused these our letters to be made patent. Witness myself at Westminster, on the eighth day of April, in the first year of our reign. Scarle.

By the King and Council in Parliament, because they are charged with the men of Derby with the making of a balinger.

4164.

XIII.—*Charter of King Henry IV.*
1399, November 18.

HENRY IV.

HENRICUS, Dei gratia, Rex Angliae et Franciae, et Dominus Hiberniae, archiepiscopis, episcopis, abbatibus, prioribus, ducibus, comitibus, baronibus, justitiariis, vicecomitibus, praepositis, ministris, et omnibus ballivis et fidelibus suis, salutem.

Recital and confirmation of previous charters.

[I]nspeximus litteras patentes Domini Ricardi, nuper Regis Angliae, Secundi post Conquaestum, factas in haec verba : 'RICARDUS, Dei gratia' [*etc., reciting Charter of Richard II., No. XII.*]. Nos autem, omnes et singulas concessiones, confirmationes et restitutiones praedictas ratas habentes et gratas, eas, pro nobis et heredibus nostris, quantum in nobis est, acceptamus, approbamus, ratificamus, ac dilectis nobis Burgensibus villae praedictae, heredibus et successoribus suis, Burgensibus ejusdem villae, concedimus et confirmamus, sicut cartae praedictae rationabiliter testantur.

Liberties shall not be forfeited by non-user.

Praeterea, volentes eisdem Burgensibus gratiam facere ampliorem, de gratia nostra speciali, concessimus, pro nobis et heredibus nostris, quantum in nobis est, eisdem Burgensibus, quod, licet ipsi vel antecessores sui aliqua vel aliquibus libertatum vel quietantiarum in cartis praedictis contentarum, aliquo casu emergente, plene usi non fuerint, ipsi tamen, et eorum heredes et successores, libertatibus et quietantiis praedictis, et earum qualibet, de cetero plene gaudeant et utantur, sine occasione vel impedimento nostri vel heredum nostrorum, justitiariorum, escaëtorum, vicecomitum, ac aliorum ballivorum et ministrorum nostrorum et heredum nostrorum quorumcumque.

Grant of cognizance of all pleas relating to lands, etc., in the Borough, trespasses, etc.;

Nos insuper, volentes nunc Majorem et Ballivos ac Burgenses villae praedictae, necnon eorum heredes et successores, suis multimodis exigentibus meritis, favore prosequi uberiori, de gratia nostra speciali, ex certa scientia nostra, et de assensu Consilii nostri, concessimus, pro nobis et heredibus nostris, et hac carta nostra confirmavimus, praefatis Majori, Ballivis et Burgensibus, quod ipsi et eorum heredes et successores imperpetuum habeant infra villam praedictam cognitiones omnium placitorum per Majorem et Ballivos ejusdem villae pro tempore existentes, seu alios, quos ad hoc deputaverint, tenendorum, tam videlicet de terris, tenementis et redditibus infra libertatem villae

XIII.—*Charter of King Henry IV.*
1399, November 18.

HENRY, by the grace of God, King of England and France, and Lord of Ireland, to his archbishops, bishops, abbots, priors, dukes, earls, barons, justices, sheriffs, reeves, ministers, and all his bailiffs and faithful subjects, greeting. *(HENRY IV.)*

We have inspected the letters patent of Lord Richard, late King of England, the Second after the Conquest, made in these words: 'RICHARD, by the grace of God' [*etc., reciting Charter of Richard II., No. XII.*]. We, esteeming all and singular the aforesaid grants, confirmations and restitutions as valid and acceptable, do accept, approve, ratify, and grant and confirm them, for us and our heirs, so far as in us lies, to our well-beloved Burgesses of the town aforesaid, their heirs and successors, Burgesses of the same town, as the charters aforesaid do reasonably witness. *(Recital and confirmation of previous charters.)*

Moreover, we, desiring to show the same Burgesses greater favour, have granted, of our especial grace, for us and our heirs, so far as in us lies, to the same Burgesses, that, although they or their ancestors may not have fully used, on any opportunity occurring, any one or more of the liberties or acquittances in the aforesaid charters contained, nevertheless they, and their heirs and successors, may henceforth fully enjoy and use the liberties and acquittances aforesaid, and each of them, without hindrance or impediment from us or our heirs, justices, escheators, sheriffs, and others the bailiffs and ministers of us and our heirs whatsoever. *(Liberties shall not be forfeited by non-user.)*

We moreover, wishing to bestow more ample favour upon the present Mayor and Bailiffs and Burgesses of the town aforesaid, as well as their heirs and successors, on account of their manifold deserts, have granted, for us and our heirs, of our especial grace, of our certain knowledge, and with the assent of our Council, and by this our charter have confirmed, to the aforesaid Mayor, Bailiffs and Burgesses, that they and their heirs and successors for ever shall have cognizance of all pleas within the aforesaid town, to be held by the Mayor and Bailiffs of the same town for the time being, or by others whom they shall depute for this purpose, to wit, as well of lands, tenements and *(Grant of cognizance of all pleas relating to lands, etc., in the Borough, trespasses, etc.;)*

Henry IV.

and of pleas of assize of tenures in the Borough.

praedictae existentibus, quam de transgressionibus, conventionibus, contractibus, negotiis et querelis quibuscumque, infra libertatem praedictam ac procinctum ejusdem villae emergentibus sive factis, de quibuscumque tenentibus et residentibus infra feodum villae praedictae; ac etiam placitorum assisarum de tenuris infra eandem libertatem, quas coram Justitiariis nostris vel heredum nostrorum ad assisas in Comitatu Notyngham' capiendas assignatis arramiari contigerit: et quod Justitiarii ipsi, cum cognitiones placitorum earundem assisarum ex parte dictorum Majoris, Ballivorum et Burgensium debito modo petitae fuerint, hoc eis sine difficultate allocent, et brevia originalia et processus, si qui inde habiti fuerint, praefatis Majori et Ballivis, aut aliis ad dicta placita tenenda, ut praemittitur, deputatis, faciant liberari.

Grant of chattels of felons and fugitives.

Et quod praedicti Major, Ballivi et Burgenses, ac heredes et successores sui imperpetuum, habeant catalla felonum et fugitivorum de tenentibus et residentibus infra libertatem praedictam, ita quod si quis eorum pro delicto suo vitam vel membrum debeat amittere, vel fugerit et judicio stare noluerit, vel aliud quodcumque delictum fecerit pro quo catalla sua debeat perdere, ubicumque justitia de eo fieri debeat, sive in Curia nostra vel heredum nostrorum, sive in alia Curia, ipsa catalla sint praedictorum Majoris, Ballivorum et Burgensium, ac heredum et successorum suorum; et quod liceat eis seu ministris suis, sine impedimento nostri vel heredum nostrorum, vicecomitum aut aliorum ballivorum seu ministrorum nostrorum quorumcumque, ponere se in scisinam de catallis praedictis, et ea ad usum praedictorum Majoris, Ballivorum et Burgensium, heredum et successorum suorum, retinere.

Grant of all fines and amercements, year day and waste, and other forfeitures, forfeited before any Judges whatsoever.

Et quod habeant imperpetuum omnes fines pro transgressionibus et aliis delictis quibuscumque, ac etiam fines pro licentia concordandi, ac omnia amerciamenta, redemptiones, et exitus forisfactos, forisfacturas, annum diem vastum et streppum, et omnia, quae ad nos et heredes nostros pertinere poterunt de hujusmodi anno die et vasto, et murdris, de omnibus hominibus et tenentibus villae praedictae, in quibuscumque Curiis nostris et heredum nostrorum homines et tenentes illos, tam coram nobis et heredibus nostris, et in Cancellaria nostra et heredum nostrorum, ac coram Thesaurario et Baronibus nostris et heredum

rents being within the liberty of the town aforesaid, as of tres- HENRY IV.
passes, covenants, contracts, affairs and cases whatsoever, arising
or done within the liberty aforesaid and the precinct of the
same town, of whatsoever tenants and residents within the fee
of the aforesaid town; and also of pleas of assizes of tenures and of pleas
within the same liberty that shall happen to be arraıned before of assize of tenures in the
the Justices of us or our heirs assigned to take assizes in the Borough.
County of Nottingham: and that the same Justices, when
cognizance of the said pleas of assizes has been sought in proper
manner on behalf of the said Mayor, Bailiffs and Burgesses,
shall without difficulty allow this to them, and shall cause the
original writs and the processes, if any such have been had, to
be delivered to the aforesaid Mayor and Bailiffs, or to others
deputed, as is aforesaid, to hold the said pleas.

And that the aforesaid Mayor, Bailiffs and Burgesses, and Grant of chat-
their heirs and successors for ever, shall have the chattels of tels of felons and fugitives.
felons and fugitives from the tenants and residents within the
liberty aforesaid, so that if any one of them for his crime ought
to lose life or member, or have fled and have not abided judgment, or have committed any other offence for which he ought
to lose his chattels, wheresoever justice ought to be done upon
him, either in the Court of us or of our heirs, or in another
Court, the said chattels shall be the property of the aforesaid
Mayor, Bailiffs and Burgesses, and of their heirs and successors;
and that it shall be lawful for them or their officers to put themselves in seisin of the chattels aforesaid, without hindrance from
us or our heirs, our sheriffs or others our bailiffs or officers whatsoever, and to retain them for the use of the aforesaid Mayor,
Bailiffs and Burgesses, their heirs and successors.

And that they shall have for ever all fines for trespasses and Grant of all
other offences whatsoever, and also fines for licence to agree, fines and amercements,
and all other amercements, ransoms, and forfeited issues, for- year day and waste, and
feitures, year day waste and estrepment, and all other things other for-
that may pertain to us and our heirs of such year day and waste, feited before
and of murders, of all men and tenants of the town aforesaid, any Judges whatsoever.
in whatsoever Courts of us or our heirs it shall happen that the
said men and tenants shall be adjudged to make fines, or be
amerced, or to forfeit issues, year day and waste, or forfeitures
and murders, as well before us and our heirs, and in the

HENRY IV. nostrorum de Scaccario, et coram Justitiariis nostris et heredum nostrorum de Banco, et coram Senescallo et Marescallo seu Clerico Mercati Hospitii nostri et heredum nostrorum, qui pro tempore fuerint, et in aliis Curiis nostris et heredum nostrorum, quam coram Justitiariis Itinerantibus ad Communia Placita et ad Placita Forestae, et quibuscumque aliis Justitiariis et ministris nostris et heredum nostrorum, tam in praesentia nostra et heredum nostrorum, quam in absentia nostra et heredum nostrorum, fines facere, vel amerciari, exitus forisfacere, annum diem et vastum, seu forisfacturas et murdra, adjudicari contigerit; quae fines, amerciamenta, redemptiones, exitus, annus dies vastum sive streppum, forisfacturae et murdra ad nos vel heredes nostros possent pertinere si praefatis Majori, Ballivis et Burgensibus concessa non fuissent: ita quod ipsi per se vel per ballivos et ministros suos fines, amerciamenta, redemptiones, exitus, et forisfacturas hujusmodi hominum et tenentium praedictorum, et omnia, quae ad nos et heredes nostros pertinere possint de anno die et vasto sive streppo, et murdris praedictis levare, percipere et habere possint, sine occasione vel impedimento nostri vel heredum nostrorum, justitiariorum, escaëtorum, vicecomitum, coronatorum, aut aliorum ballivorum seu ministrorum nostrorum quorumcumque.

Grant of return of all writs. Et etiam, quod praedicti Major, Ballivi et Burgenses, ac heredes et successores sui, imperpetuum habeant retorna omnium brevium nostrorum et heredum nostrorum, ac summonitionum de Scaccario nostro et heredum nostrorum, et attachiamenta tam de placitis Coronae quam de aliis quibuscumque in terris et feodis villae praedictae, ac executiones eorundem brevium et summonitionum, de omnibus, quae infra libertatem praedictam emergent; ita quod nullus vicecomes aut alius ballivus seu minister noster vel heredum nostrorum libertatem praedictam ingrediatur ad executiones eorundem brevium et summonitionum, seu ad attachiamenta de placitis Coronae vel aliis praedictis, aut aliquod aliud officium ibidem faciendum, nisi in defectu ipsorum Majoris, Ballivorum et Burgensium, heredum vel successorum suorum.

Licence to approve themselves of all purprestures and wastes. Concessimus etiam, pro nobis et heredibus nostris, ex certa scientia nostra, et de assensu praedicto, eisdem Majori, Ballivis et Burgensibus, ac eorum heredibus et successoribus, quod ipsi se

Chancery of us and our heirs, and before the Treasurer and Barons of us and our heirs of the Exchequer, and before the Justices of us and our heirs of the Bench, and before the Steward and Marshall or Clerk of the Market of the Household of us and our heirs, for the time being, and in other the Courts of us and our heirs, as before the Justices in Eyre for Common Pleas and for Pleas of the Forest, and before other Justices and officers whatsoever of us and of our heirs, as well in the presence of us and of our heirs, as in the absence of us and of our heirs; which fines, amercements, ransoms, issues, year day waste or estrepment, forfeitures and murders might pertain to us or our heirs if they had not been granted to the aforesaid Mayor, Bailiffs and Burgesses: so that they by themselves or by their bailiffs and officers may levy, receive and have the fines, amercements, ransoms, issues, and forfeitures of such aforesaid men and tenants, and all things that may pertain to us and our heirs of the aforesaid year day and waste or estrepment, and murders, without let or hindrance from us or our heirs, justices, escheators, sheriffs, coroners, or others our bailiffs or officers whatsoever.

And also, that the aforesaid Mayor, Bailiffs and Burgesses, and their heirs and successors, shall have for ever the returns of all the writs of us and of our heirs, and of summonses of the Exchequer of us and of our heirs, and attachments both of pleas of the Crown and of other things whatsoever in the lands and fees of the aforesaid town, and executions of the same writs and summonses, of all things that shall arise within the aforesaid liberty; so that no sheriff or other bailiff or officer of us or of our heirs shall enter the aforesaid liberty to make execution of those writs and summonses, or attachments of pleas of the Crown or of the other things aforesaid, or any other duty there, except in default of the said Mayor, Bailiffs and Burgesses, their heirs or successors. *Grant of return of all writs.*

We have also granted, for us and our heirs, of our certain knowledge, and with the assent aforesaid, to the same Mayor, Bailiffs and Burgesses, and their heirs and successors, that they *Licence to approve themselves of all purprestures and wastes.*

appruare et commodum suum facere possint de omnibus pur-
presturis, tam in terris quam in aquis, factis vel faciendis, et de
omnibus vastis infra limites et bundas villae praedictae, in supportationem onerum infra villam praedictam in dies emergentium.

Power to hear and determine all pleas pertaining to Justices of the Peace, of Labourers and Artizans.
Ac etiam, quod ipsi, et heredes ac successores sui praedicti,
habeant imperpetuum plenam correctionem, punitionem, auctoritatem et potestatem ad inquirendum, audiendum et terminandum per Majorem et Recordatorem villae praedictae ac alios
quatuor probiores et legaliores homines villae praedictae, per
Majorem ejusdem villae pro tempore existentem eligendos, et
successores suos imperpetuum, omnes materias, querelas, defectus, causas et articulos, qui ad officium Justitiarii Pacis, Laboratorum et Artificum pertinent, ac alias res quascumque infra
dictam villam et suburbia ejusdem emergentes vel contingentes,
et qui aliquo modo coram Justitiario Pacis, Laboratorum et
Artificum inquiri poterunt et terminari, adeo plene et integre
sicut Justitiarii Pacis, Laboratorum et Artificum in Comitatu
Notyngham' ante haec tempora habuerunt vel excercuerunt;

County Justices not to intermeddle in any pleas in the Borough.
absque eo, quod Justitiarii Pacis, Laboratorum et Artificum
nostri et heredum nostrorum, in Comitatu praedicto se imposterum aliqualiter intromittant de aliquibus rebus, causis, querelis,
materiis, defectibus seu aliis articulis quibuscumque ad Justitiarios Pacis, Laboratorum et Artificum spectantibus sive pertinentibus, infra villam praedictam et suburbia ejusdem ex quacumque

The Burgesses shall not determine any felony without royal licence.
causa emergentibus sive contingentibus: ita quod praedicti
Major et Recordator ac praedicti quatuor probiores et legaliores
homines ejusdem villae, qui pro tempore fuerint, ad determin-
ationem alicujus feloniae absque aliquo speciali mandato nostro

Grant of all profits from above jurisdiction.
vel heredum nostrorum quoquo modo non procedant: et quod
praedicti Major, Ballivi et Burgenses, ac heredes et successores
sui imperpetuum, habeant omnes fines et amerciamenta, exitus
et proficua de eadem justitiaria provenientia, adeo integre sicut
Major, Ballivi et Burgenses villae de Coventre hujus[modi] fines,
amerciamenta, exitus et proficua ante sextum diem Aprilis,
anno regni praedicti Ricardi nuper Regis vicesimo secundo,
virtute cartarum Regum Angliae eis inde confectarum et per
ipsum nuper Regem confirmatarum optinuerunt.

No arrays of men to be made without
Et insuper, quod quandocumque aliqua arraiatio hominum
ad arma, hominum armatorum, hobelariorum, aut sagittariorum

may approve and make their profit of all purprestures made or to be made, both on lands and in waters, and of all wastes within the limits and bounds of the town aforesaid, for the support of the burdens daily arising within the town aforesaid.

And also that they, and their heirs and successors aforesaid, shall have for ever full correction, punishment, authority and power as fully and wholly as Justices of the Peace, of Labourers and of Artificers have had or have exercised before this time in the County of Nottingham, to inquire, hear and determine by the Mayor and Recorder of the town aforesaid and four other upright and lawful men of the town aforesaid, to be selected by the Mayor of the same town for the time being, and their successors for ever, all matters, plaints, defaults, causes and articles that pertain to the office of a Justice of the Peace, of Labourers and of Artificers, and all other matters whatsoever arising or happening within the said town and the suburbs of the same, and that might be inquired and determined in any wise before a Justice of the Peace, of Labourers and of Artificers; without the Justices of the Peace, of Labourers and of Artificers of us and our heirs, in the County aforesaid hereafter in any wise interfering with any matters, causes, plaints, cases, defaults or other articles whatsoever from whatsoever cause arising or happening within the town aforesaid and the suburbs of the same, belonging or pertaining to Justices of the Peace, of Labourers and of Artificers: provided that the aforesaid Mayor and Recorder and the aforesaid four upright and lawful men of the same town, for the time being, do not proceed in any wise to the determination of any felony without some special mandate of us or of our heirs: and that the aforesaid Mayor, Bailiffs and Burgesses, and their heirs and successors for ever, shall have all fines and amercements, issues and profits arising from the same justice-ship, as fully as the Mayor, Bailiffs and Burgesses of the town of Coventry have obtained such fines, amercements, issues and profits before the sixth day of April, in the twenty-second year of the reign of the aforesaid Richard the late King, by virtue of the charters of the Kings of England thereof made to them and confirmed by the same late King.

And moreover, that whenever any array of men-at-arms, armed men, hobelers, or archers shall be made hereafter in the

Henry IV.

Power to hear and determine all pleas pertaining to Justices of the Peace, of Labourers and Artizans.

County Justices not to intermeddle in any pleas in the Borough.

The Burgesses shall not determine any felony without royal licence.

Grant of all profits from above jurisdiction.

No arrays of men to be made without

HENRY IV.

the Mayor being joined in the commission.

They may enjoy all liberties in as ample manner as any of their predecessors have done.

fiet ex nunc in dicta villa de Notyngham virtute commissionis seu aliorum mandatorum nostrorum vel heredum nostrorum sub aliquo sigillorum nostrorum vel heredum nostrorum, Major villae praedictae pro tempore existens ipsis, qui per nos et heredes nostros ad hoc assignati fuerint, ad arraiationem illam faciendam per commissiones et mandata hujusmodi sit adjunctus; et quod sine adjunctione illa nulla arraiatio hominum ad arma, hominum armatorum, hobelariorum, aut sagittariorum in eadem villa fiat quoquo modo.

Volumus etiam et concedimus, pro nobis et heredibus nostris, de assensu praedicto, quod per aliquam causam aut colorem aliquae vel aliqua de franchesiis, libertatibus, privilegiis, immunitatibus, quietantiis, seu commoditatibus praefatis Majori, Ballivis et Burgensibus de Notyngham, et successoribus suis, per progenitores nostros ante haec tempora concessis, et per nos confirmatis, erga nunc Majorem, Ballivos vel Burgenses ejusdem villae de Notyngham, seu heredes vel successores suos, nullo modo denegentur, restringantur, minuantur nec abbrevientur; set quod iidem Major, Ballivi et Burgenses dictae villae de Notyngham, ac eorum heredes et successores, habeant, teneant et excerceant omnia alia et singula franchesias, libertates, privilegia, immunitates, quietantias et commoditates, ac consuetudines, et eis et eorum quolibet plene gaudeant et utantur, de articulo in articulum ac de verbo in verbum, quae et prout Major, Ballivi et Burgenses praedictae villae de Notyngham, ac antecessores et praedecessores sui, habuerunt et excercuerunt ex concessione et confirmatione dictorum progenitorum nostrorum ante haec tempora, imperpetuum.

Hiis testibus: venerabilibus patribus Thoma Cantuariensi, totius Angliae Primate, Ricardo Eboracensi, Angliae Primate, Archiepiscopis, Roberto Londoniensi, Willelmo Wyntoniensi, Johanne Eliensi, Henrico Lincolniensi, Episcopis; Edmundo Duce Eboracensi avunculo nostro carissimo; Thoma Warr[ewyck'], Henrico Northumb[erland'], Radulpho Westmerland', Comitibus; Johanne de Scarle Cancellario, Johanne Norbury Thesaurario nostris; Willelmo de Roos, de Hamelak; Willelmo de Wilughby; Johanne de Cobham; Thoma Erpyngham, Camerario nostro; Thoma Rempston, Senescallo Hospitii nostri; Magistro Ricardo de Clifford, Custode Privati Sigilli nostri, et

said town of Nottingham by virtue of a commission or other mandates of us or of our heirs under any of the seals of us or of our heirs, the Mayor of the town aforesaid for the time being shall be joined by such commissions and mandates to those who shall be assigned for this purpose by us and our heirs, to make that array; and that without such joining no array of men-at-arms, armed men, hobelers, or archers shall be made in any wise in the same town.

HENRY IV.
the Mayor being joined in the commission.

We do also will and grant, for us and our heirs, with the assent aforesaid, that any of the franchises, liberties, privileges, immunities, acquittances, or benefits granted before this time by our progenitors to the aforesaid Mayor, Bailiffs and Burgesses of Nottingham, and their successors, and by us confirmed, shall not in any wise be denied, restrained, diminished or abridged for any cause or pretext, in respect to the present Mayor, Bailiffs or Burgesses of the same town of Nottingham, or their heirs or successors; but that the same Mayor, Bailiffs and Burgesses of the said town of Nottingham, and their heirs and successors, shall have, hold and exercise for ever all and singular the other franchises, liberties, privileges, immunities, acquittances, and benefits, and customs, and shall fully enjoy and use each and all of them, article by article and word by word, in the same manner as the Mayor, Bailiffs and Burgesses of the aforesaid town of Nottingham, and their ancestors and predecessors, have had and exercised before this time by the grant and confirmation of our said progenitors.

They may enjoy all liberties in as ample manner as any of their predecessors have done.

These being witnesses: the venerable fathers Thomas, Archbishop of Canterbury, Primate of all England; Richard, Archbishop of York, Primate of England; Robert, Bishop of London; William, Bishop of Winchester; John, Bishop of Ely; Henry, Bishop of Lincoln; Edmund, Duke of York, our dearest uncle; Thomas, Earl of Warwick; Henry, Earl of Northumberland; Ralph, Earl of Westmoreland; John de Scarle, our Chancellor; John Norbury, our Treasurer; William de Roos, of Hamelak; William de Willoughby; John de Cobham; Thomas Erpingham, our Chamberlain; Thomas Rempston, Steward of our Household; Master Richard de Clifford, Keeper of our Privy Seal, and

HENRY IV.   aliis. Datum per manum nostram apud Westmonasterium, decimo octavo die Novembris, anno regni nostri primo.
Per ipsum Regem.   Wakeryng.
                                                      4166.

XIV.—*Charter of King Henry V.*
1414, May 24.

HENRY V.   [1]HENRICUS, Dei gratia, Rex Angliae et Franciae, et Dominus Hiberniae, archiepiscopis, episcopis, abbatibus, prioribus, ducibus, comitibus, baronibus, justitiariis, vicecomitibus, praepositis, ministris, et omnibus ballivis et fidelibus suis, salutem.[2]

Inspeximus cartam Domini Henrici, nuper Regis Angliae, patris nostri, factam in haec verba: 'HENRICUS, Dei gratia' [*etc., reciting Charter of King Henry IV., No. XIII.*].

Confirmation of previous charters.   Nos autem, omnes et singulas concessiones, confirmationes et restitutiones praedictas ratas habentes et gratas, eas, pro nobis et heredibus nostris, quantum in nobis est, acceptamus, approbamus, ratificamus, ac dilectis nobis nunc Majori, Ballivis et Burgensibus villae praedictae, heredibus et successoribus suis, tenore praesentium concedimus et confirmamus, sicut cartae praedictae rationabiliter testantur, et prout iidem Major, Ballivi et Burgenses villae praedictae libertatibus et quietantiis praedictis uti et gaudere debent, ipsique et antecessores sui, Majores, Ballivi et Burgenses ejusdem villae libertatibus et quietantiis illis a tempore confectionis cartarum praedictarum rationabiliter uti et gaudere consueverunt.

In cujus rei testimonium has litteras nostras fieri fecimus patentes.[3] Teste me ipso apud Leycestr', vicesimo quarto die Maii, anno regni nostri secundo.

                      Pro decem libris solutis in Hanaperio.[4]

XV.—*Charter of King Henry VI.*
1448, June 28.

HENRY VI.   REX omnibus, ad quos, etc., salutem. Inspeximus cartam Domini Henrici, nuper Regis Angliae, patris nostri, factam in

---

[1] This is taken from the enrolment on the Patent Roll, 2 Hen. V., pars 1, m. 24, and from the recital of this charter in the confirmatory Charter of King Henry VI.

[2] The Patent Roll reads: 'Rex omnibus, ad quos, etc., salutem' (=the King to all to whom, etc.), the usual abridgment in enrolments of the above compellation.

others. Given by our hand at Westminster, the eighteenth day of November, in the first year of our reign.

By the King himself. Wakering.

4166.

XIV.—*Charter of King Henry V.*
1414, May 24.

¹HENRY, by the grace of God, King of England and France, and Lord of Ireland, to his archbishops, bishops, abbots, priors, dukes, earls, barons, justices, sheriffs, reeves, ministers, and all his bailiffs and faithful subjects, greeting.²

We have inspected the charter of the Lord Henry, late King of England, our father, made in these words: 'HENRY, by the grace of God' [*etc., reciting Charter of King Henry IV., No. XIII.*].

We, esteeming all and singular the aforesaid grants, confirmations and restitutions as valid and agreeable to us, do accept, approve, ratify, and by the tenor of these presents do grant and confirm them, for us and our heirs, so far as in us lies, to our well-beloved the present Mayor, Bailiffs and Burgesses of the town aforesaid, their heirs and successors, as the charters aforesaid do reasonably witness, and as the same Mayor, Bailiffs and Burgesses of the town aforesaid ought to use and enjoy the liberties and acquittances aforesaid, and as they and their ancestors, Mayors, Bailiffs and Burgesses of the same town were wont to reasonably use and enjoy those liberties and acquittances from the time of the making of the charters aforesaid.

In witness whereof we have caused these our letters to be made patent.³ Witness myself at Leicester, the twenty-fourth day of May, in the second year of our reign.

For ten pounds paid into the Hanaper.⁴

XV.—*Charter of King Henry VI.*
1448, June 28.

THE KING to all to whom, etc., greeting. We have seen the charter of the Lord Henry, late King of England, our father,

---

³ The Patent Roll reads: 'In cujus, etc. Teste Rege apud Leycestr', xxiiij. die Maii.'

⁴ From the Patent Roll.

HENRY VI. haec verba: 'HENRICUS, Dei gratia' [*etc., reciting Charter of King Henry V., No. XIV.*].

Confirmation of previous charters.

Nos autem, omnia et singula franchesias, libertates, privilegia, quietantias, immunitates, concessiones, confirmationes et restitutiones praedicta rata habentes et grata, ea, pro nobis, heredibus et successoribus nostris, quantum in nobis est, acceptamus, approbamus et ratificamus, ac omnia et singula franchesias, libertates, privilegia, quietantias et immunitates praedicta dilectis nobis nunc Majori, Ballivis et Burgensibus villae praedictae, heredibus et successoribus suis, tenore praesentium concedimus et confirmamus, sicut cartae praedictae rationabiliter testantur et prout iidem Major, Ballivi et Burgenses ejusdem villae Notyngham' vel praedecessores sui unquam franchesiis, libertatibus, privilegiis, quietantiis et immunitatibus praedictis uti et gaudere debent, potuerunt seu debuerunt, ipsique vel praedecessores sui franchesiis, libertatibus, privilegiis, quietantiis et immunitatibus illis unquam post confectionem cartarum praedictarum rationabiliter uti et gaudere consueverunt, potuerunt vel debuerunt; licet dicti nunc Major, Ballivi et Burgenses ejusdem villae vel praedecessores sui franchesiis, libertatibus, privilegiis, quietantiis et immunitatibus praedictis seu eorum aliquo abusi vel non usi fuerint.

Incorporation of the Borough.

Et ulterius, de uberiori gratia nostra, ex mero motu et certa scientia nostris, concessimus, et per praesentes confirmamus pro nobis, heredibus et successoribus nostris, nunc Burgensibus ejusdem villae Notyngham' (quae est et a diu extitit villa sub certa forma corporata), ac eorundem Burgensium heredibus et successoribus, Burgensibus ipsius villae, imperpetuum, quod villa illa de Majore et Burgensibus ex nunc imperpetuum sit corporata; et quod iidem Major et Burgenses, et successores sui, Majores et Burgenses villae illius sic corporatae, sint una communitas perpetua corporata in re et nomine per nomen Majoris et Burgensium villae Notyngham'; habeantque successionem perpetuam; et quod Major et Burgenses villae illius, et successores sui praedicti, per idem nomen sint habiles et capaces in lege ad omnimoda placita, sectas, querelas et demandas, necnon actiones reales, personales, et mixtas quascumque per ipsos seu contra ipsos mota seu movenda in quibuscumque Curiis nostris, heredum vel successorum nostrorum, aut aliorum quorumcumque, tam

made in these words: 'HENRY, by the grace of God' [*etc.*, *reciting Charter of King Henry V., No. XIV.*].   HENRY VI.

We also, considering all and singular the franchises, liberties, privileges, acquittances, immunities, concessions, confirmations and restitutions aforesaid as valid and acceptable, do, for us, our heirs and successors, so far as in us lies, accept, approve and ratify them, and do grant and confirm all and singular the franchises, liberties, privileges, acquittances and immunities aforesaid to our well-beloved the present Mayor, Bailiffs and Burgesses of the town aforesaid, their heirs and successors, by the tenor of these presents, as the charters aforesaid do reasonably witness, and as the same Mayor, Bailiffs and Burgesses of the same town of Nottingham or their predecessors at any time ought, might or should use and enjoy the franchises, liberties, privileges, acquittances and immunities aforesaid, and as they or their predecessors have been accustomed to, might or should have reasonably used and enjoyed those franchises, liberties, privileges, acquittances and immunities at any time after the making of the charters aforesaid; although the said present Mayor, Bailiffs and Burgesses of the same town or their predecessors may have abused or not used the franchises, liberties, privileges, acquittances and immunities aforesaid or any of them. Confirmation of previous charters.

And furthermore, of our more abundant grace, of our mere motion and certain knowledge, we have granted, and by these presents we do confirm for us, our heirs and successors, to the present Burgesses of the same town of Nottingham (which is and for a long time has been a town incorporated under a certain form), and to the heirs and successors of the same Burgesses, Burgesses of the same town, for ever, that that town shall henceforth for ever be incorporated of a Mayor and Burgesses; and that the same Mayor and Burgesses, and their successors, Mayors and Burgesses of that town so incorporated, shall be a perpetual incorporated community in fact and in name by the name of the Mayor and Burgesses of the town of Nottingham; and that they shall have a perpetual succession; and that the Mayor and Burgesses of that town, and their successors aforesaid, shall be able and capable in law by that name to prosecute and defend all manner of pleas, suits, plaints and demands, and also actions real, personal, and mixed whatsoever Incorporation of the Borough.

coram nobis, heredibus vel successoribus nostris, ubicumque fuerimus, et coram nobis, heredibus et successoribus nostris, in Cancellaria nostra, heredum et successorum nostrorum, quam coram quibuscumque Justitiariis et Judicibus spiritualibus et saecularibus prosequenda et defendenda; et quod in eisdem placitare possint et placitari, respondere et responderi: et quod Major et Burgenses ejusdem villae, et successores sui, per idem nomen terras, tenementa, possessiones, et hereditamenta quaecumque adquirere possint, tenere sibi et successoribus suis, imperpetuum.

The Borough erected into a County.
Et insuper, de habundantiori gratia nostra, ex mero motu et certa scientia nostris, concessimus, pro nobis, heredibus et successoribus nostris, praedictis nunc Burgensibus villae illius, et successoribus suis, Burgensibus ejusdem villae, imperpetuum, quod eadem villa Notyngham' ac procinctus ejusdem prout se extendunt vel utuntur, qui infra corpus Comitatus Notyngham' jam existunt et continentur, ab eodem Comitatu a quinto decimo die mensis Septembris proximo futuro separati, distincti, divisi, et in omnibus penitus exempti existant imperpetuum, tam per
The King's Hall excepted from the County of the Borough.
terram quam per aquam,—Castro nostro Notyngham' et mesuagio nostro vocato '*le Kyngeshall*,' in quo est gaola nostra Comitatuum nostrorum Notyngham' et Derb[iae], tantummodo exceptis,— et quod eadem villa Notyngham' et procinctus ejusdem prout se extendunt vel utuntur, exceptis prae-exceptis, sint ab eodem die Comitatus per se, et non parcella dicti Comitatus Notyngham'; et quod eadem villa Notyngham' et procinctus ejusdem prout se extendunt vel utuntur, exceptis prae-exceptis, Comitatus villae Notyngham' per se imperpetuum nuncupentur, teneantur et habeantur.

The Burgesses may elect two Sheriffs in place of two Bailiffs.
Et quod dicti nunc Burgenses ejusdem villae, et successores sui, Burgenses villae illius, imperpetuum, loco duorum Ballivorum ejusdem villae, habeant duos Vicecomites in eisdem villa et procinctu de se ipsis eligendos, necnon Vicecomitatum ejusdem villae et procinctu[u]m ejusdem villae prout se extendunt vel utuntur, exceptis prae-exceptis; qui quidem Vicecomites in forma subscripta eligentur et perficientur, videlicet, Major et Burgenses villae illius, loco duorum Ballivorum ejusdem villae,

moved or to be moved by them or against them in whatsoever HENRY VI.
the Courts of us, our heirs or our successors, or of any others
whatsoever, as well before us, our heirs or successors, wheresoever we may be, and before us, our heirs and successors, in the
Chancery of us, our heirs and successors, as well as before whatsoever Justices and Judges spiritual and temporal; and that
they may plead and be impleaded, answer and be answered in
the same: and that the Mayor and Burgesses of the same town,
and their successors, may acquire by the same name lands, tenements, possessions, and hereditaments whatsoever, to hold to
them and their successors, for ever.

And furthermore, of our more abundant grace, of our mere The Borough erected into a County.
motion and certain knowledge, we have granted, for us, our heirs
and successors, to the aforesaid present Burgesses of that town,
and to their successors, Burgesses of the same town, for ever,
that the same town of Nottingham and the precincts thereof as
they extend or are used, which now exist and are contained
within the body of the County of Nottingham, shall be for ever
separated, distinct, divided, and in everything utterly exempt, as
well by land as by water, from the same County from the
fifteenth day of the month of September next to come,—our The King's Hall excepted from the County of the Borough.
Castle of Nottingham and our messuage called 'the King's
Hall,' wherein is our gaol for our Counties of Nottingham and
Derby, being alone excepted,—and that the same town of Nottingham and the precincts thereof as they extend or are used,
except as before-excepted, shall be from the same day a County
by itself, and not a parcel of the said County of Nottingham;
and that the same County of Nottingham and the precincts
thereof as they extend or are used, except as before-excepted,
shall be called, held and esteemed the County of the town of
Nottingham by itself for ever.

And that the said present Burgesses of the same town, and The Burgesses may elect two Sheriffs in place of two Bailiffs.
their successors, Burgesses of that town, for ever, shall have, in
the stead of the two Bailiffs of the same town, two Sheriffs
in the same town and precinct to be chosen from themselves,
and also the Shrievalty of the same town and of the precincts of
the same town as they extend or are used, except as before-
excepted; which Sheriffs shall be chosen and made in the form
underwritten, to wit, the Mayor and Burgesses of that town shall

CHARTER OF HENRY VI. [1448]

HENRY VI.

eligent, in dicto quinto decimo die mensis Septembris proximo futuro, de se ipsis duos Burgenses ejusdem villae in Vicecomites villae illius et procinctu[u]m ejusdem villae prout se extendunt vel utuntur, exceptis prae-exceptis; qui quidem Vicecomites habeant et occupent officium Vicecomitatus ejusdem villae et procinctu[u]m ejusdem villae prout se extendunt vel utuntur, exceptis prae-exceptis, usque diem Sancti Michaëlis Archangeli tunc proximo futurum, et per eundem diem quousque in eodem die alii duo Burgenses ejusdem villae in Vicecomites villae illius et procinctu[u]m ejusdem villae prout se extendunt vel utuntur, exceptis prae-exceptis, pro anno tunc proximo futuro per tunc

Such Sheriffs to be elected annually.

Majorem et Burgenses villae illius eligantur. Et quod ex tunc Vicecomites villae illius et procinctu[u]m ejusdem villae prout se extendunt vel utuntur, exceptis prae-exceptis, annuatim imperpetuum in festo Sancti Michaëlis Archangeli eligentur et perficientur in forma subscripta, videlicet, Major et Burgenses ejusdem villae Notyngham' pro tempore existentes quolibet anno, in loco duorum Ballivorum villae illius, eligent de se ipsis duas personas ydoneas in Vicecomites ejusdem villae et procinctu[u]m ejusdem villae prout se extendunt vel utuntur, exceptis prae-exceptis, eodem modo quo Burgenses villae illius in Ballivos ejusdem villae ante haec tempora eligi consueverunt.

The Sheriffs to take oath of office within the Borough.

Et quod Burgenses ejusdem villae in Vicecomites villae illius et procinctu[u]m ejusdem villae prout se extendunt vel utuntur, exceptis prae-exceptis, in forma praedicta eligendi, statim post electionem de se factam, sacramenta sua coram Majore villae illius, qui pro tempore fuerit, ad officium Vicecomitum Comitatus illius debite et legitime exequendum praestabunt; et quod extra eandem villam ad sacramenta sua praestanda non transi-

The names of new Sheriffs to be returned into Chancery.

bunt: quorum quidem Vicecomitum nomina sub sigillo Majoratus illius villae Notingham' in Cancellariam nostram, heredum et successorum nostrorum, annuatim infra duodecim dies electionem[1] hujusmodi proximo sequentes mittentur.

The Mayor to be Escheator within the Borough.

Et quod tam quilibet Burgensis ejusdem villae Notyngham' in Majorem villae illius imposterum eligendus eo ipso et quam citius in Majorem villae illius electus fuerit, quam nunc Major ejusdem villae sit ex nunc Escaëtor noster, heredum et

---

[1] *electionem*,] 'electionis,' MS.

[1448] CHARTER OF HENRY VI.

choose, in the stead of the two Bailiffs of the same town, on the said fifteenth day of the month of September next to come, from themselves two Burgesses of the same town as Sheriffs of that town and of the precincts of the same town as they extend or are used, except as before-excepted; which Sheriffs shall have and occupy the office of the Shrievalty of the same town and of the precincts of the same town as they extend or are used, except as before-excepted, until the day of Saint Michael the Archangel then next to come, and throughout the same day until on the same day two other Burgesses of the same town shall be chosen by the then Mayor and Burgesses of that town as Sheriffs of that town and of the precincts of the same town as they extend or are used, except as before-excepted, for the year then next to come. And that thenceforth the Sheriffs of that town and of the precincts of the same town as they extend or are used, except as before-excepted, shall be yearly for ever chosen and made at the feast of Saint Michael the Archangel in the underwritten form, that is to say, the Mayor and Burgesses of the same town of Nottingham for the time being shall choose every year, in the stead of the two Bailiffs of that town, two fit persons from themselves as Sheriffs of the same town and of the precincts of the same town as they extend or are used, except as before-excepted, in the same manner as the Burgesses of that town were wont heretofore to be chosen as Bailiffs of the same town. And that the Burgesses of the same town to be chosen in form aforesaid as Sheriffs of that town and of the precincts of the same town as they extend or are used, except as before-excepted, immediately after election of them has been made, shall take their oath before the Mayor of that town for the time being to duly and lawfully execute the office of Sheriffs of that County; and that they shall not pass out of the same town to take their oath: the names of which Sheriffs shall be yearly sent under the seal of the Mayoralty of that town of Nottingham into the Chancery of us, our heirs and successors, within twelve days next following such election.

And that as well each Burgess of the same town of Nottingham to be hereafter chosen Mayor of that town, forthwith and so soon as he have been chosen Mayor of that town, as also the present Mayor of the same town, shall be henceforth the

HENRY VI.

Such Sheriffs to be elected annually.

The Sheriffs to take oath of office within the Borough.

The names of new Sheriffs to be returned into Chancery.

The Mayor to be Escheator within the Borough.

CHARTER OF HENRY VI. [1448]

HENRY VI.

No other Escheator to be made.

The Sheriffs of the Borough shall execute all such writs, etc., within the Borough as the Sheriffs of the County have been wont to execute there.

The Sheriffs to hold their County Courts monthly.

The Burgesses may hold a Court in the Guild Hall before the Mayor and Sheriffs.

successorum nostrorum, in villa et procinctibus illis durante toto tempore quo aliquis hujusmodi Burgensis in officio Majoratus villae illius steterit; et quod nullo tempore futuro aliquis alius Escaëtor aut Vicecomes in seu de eadem villa Notyngham' et procinctibus ejusdem prout se extendunt vel utuntur, exceptis prae-exceptis, quam de Burgensibus ejusdem villae ut praedicitur fiendis, quovis modo fiant seu existant; et quod Escaetor et Vicecomites ejusdem villae, et eorum successores imperpetuum, in eadem villa et procinctibus ejusdem prout se extendunt vel utuntur, exceptis prae-exceptis, easdem habeant potestatem, jurisdictionem, auctoritatem et libertatem, et quaecumque alia ad officia Escaëtoris et Vicecomitum pertinentia, quas et quae ceteri Escaëtores et Vicecomites nostri, heredum vel successorum nostrorum, alibi infra regnum nostrum Angliae habent vel habebunt, aut habere debent seu debebunt. Et quod omnia et singula talia brevia, praecepta et mandata, qualia per Vicecomites Notyngham' seu per Ballivos ejusdem villae infra eandem villam seu procinctus ejusdem ante haec tempora quovis modo serviri seu exequi consueverunt aut debuerunt, Vicecomitibus ejusdem villae Notyngham' ex nunc in futurum pro tempore existentibus a dicto quinto decimo die mensis Septembris immediate imperpetuum dirigantur, demandentur et liberentur.

Et quod Vicecomites ejusdem villae et procinctuum ejusdem ex nunc in futurum pro tempore existentes Comitatum suum Comitatus illius villae Notyngham' infra eandem villam et procinctus ejusdem villae prout se extendunt vel utuntur, exceptis praeexceptis, per diem Lunae de mense in mensem continue teneant in futurum, eisdem modo et forma prout alii Vicecomites nostri alibi infra regnum nostrum praedictum Comitatus suos tenent, seu prout alii Vicecomites nostri, heredum et successorum nostrorum, alibi in eodem regno nostro Comitatus suos tenebunt seu tenere deberent.

Et quod iidem nunc Burgenses villae illius, et successores sui imperpetuum, habeant Curiam ibidem ad eorum libitum de omnibus et singulis contractibus, conventionibus, et transgressionibus tam contra pacem quam aliter factis, ac aliis rebus, causis et materiis quibuscumque infra eandem villam seu procinctus ejusdem villae prout se extendunt vel utuntur, exceptis praeexceptis, quovis modo emergentibus seu contingentibus, de die

Escheator of us, our heirs and successors, in that town and in those precincts during the whole time that any such Burgess remain in the office of Mayoralty of that town; and that at no time hereafter shall any other Escheator or Sheriff, other than of the Burgesses of the same town to be made as is aforesaid, in any wise be made or be within or of the same town of Nottingham and the precincts thereof as they extend or are used, except as before-excepted; and that the Escheator and Sheriffs of the same town, and their successors for ever, shall have within the same town and the precincts of the same as they extend or are used, except as before-excepted, the same power, jurisdiction, authority and liberty, and everything else pertaining to the offices of an Escheator and Sheriffs as the other Escheators and Sheriffs of us, our heirs or successors, have or shall have, or ought or should have, elsewhere within our realm of England. And that all and singular such writs, precepts and mandates as were wont or ought to have been in any wise served or executed by the Sheriffs of Nottingham or by the Bailiffs of the same town within the same town or the precincts thereof heretofore, shall be henceforth for the future from the said fifteenth day of the month of September for ever be directed, sent and delivered immediately to the Sheriffs of the same town of Nottingham for the time being. And that the Sheriffs of the same town and the precincts thereof henceforth for the future for the time being shall hold henceforth their County Court of the County of that town of Nottingham within the same town and the precincts of the same town as they extend or are used, except as before-excepted, on Monday continually from month to month, in the same manner and form as other our Sheriffs hold their County Courts elsewhere within our realm aforesaid, or as others the Sheriffs of us, our heirs and successors, shall hold or ought to hold their County Courts elsewhere within the same our realm.

And that the same present Burgesses of that town, and their successors for ever, shall have a Court there at their pleasure of all and singular contracts, covenants, and trespasses made as well against the peace as otherwise, and of other things, causes and matters whatsoever in any wise whatsoever arising or happening within the same town or the precincts of the same town as they extend or are used, except as before-excepted, to

HENRY VI.

No other Escheator to be made.

The Sheriffs of the Borough shall execute all such writs, etc., within the Borough as the Sheriffs of the County have been wont to execute there.

The Sheriffs to hold their County Courts monthly.

The Burgesses may hold a Court in the Guild Hall before the Mayor and Sheriffs.

CHARTER OF HENRY VI. [1448

HENRY VI.

Its powers defined.

in diem in Guyhalda ejusdem villae coram Majore illius villae, seu ejus locum tenente, ac Vicecomitibus ejusdem villae pro tempore existentibus tenendam. Et quod Major villae illius pro tempore existens, aut ejus locum tenens, et Vicecomites villae illius pro tempore existentes a dicto quinto decimo die mensis Septembris habeant potestatem et auctoritatem ad audienda et determinanda in Curia illa omnimoda placita, sectas, querelas, causas et demandas, necnon actiones reales, personales, et mixtas quascumque, infra eandem villam ac libertatem et procinctus ejusdem villae prout se extendunt vel utuntur, exceptis prae-exceptis, mota seu movenda, tam in praesentia nostra, heredum et successorum nostrorum, quam in absentia

The Burgesses to have all the profits of such Court.

nostra, heredum et successorum nostrorum, cum omnimodis proficuis Curiae illius ex nunc in futurum qualitercumque contingentibus seu provenientibus, Vicecomitibus ejusdem villae pro tempore existentibus ad usum suum proprium solvendis, sine occasione vel impedimento nostri, heredum vel successorum nostrorum, aut justitiariorum nostrorum, heredum vel successorum nostrorum, quorumcumque, seu Senescalli vel Marescalli Hospitii nostri, heredum seu successorum nostrorum, sive Escaëtorum, Vicecomitum, aut aliorum ballivorum vel ministrorum nostrorum, heredum vel successorum nostrorum, quorumcumque.

The Steward and Marshall of the King's Household not to interfere in the Borough.

Et quod iidem Senescallus et Marescallus de cognitionibus placitorum de hujusmodi contractibus, conventionibus, transgressionibus, rebus, causis aut materiis quibuscumque infra eandem villam seu libertatem vel procinctus ejusdem prout se extendunt vel utuntur, exceptis prae-exceptis, emergentibus vel contingentibus, se ex nunc in futurum nullatenus intromittant, nec nullus eorum ullo modo se intromittat.

The Escheator and Sheriffs may make their proffers and accounts at the Exchequer by attorneys.

Et quod dicti Escaëtor et Vicecomites ejusdem villae Notyngham' pro tempore existentes quolibet anno separatim profra sua facere et computare possint coram Thesaurario et Baronibus de Scaccario nostro, et heredum ac successorum nostrorum, per attornatos eorundem Escaëtoris et Vicecomitum illius villae ad hoc separatim deputatos et deputandos per litteras patentes sub sigillis officiorum eorundem Escaëtoris et Vicecomitum illius villae signandas, de quibuscumque rebus officia Escaëtoris et Vicecomitum ejusdem villae tangentibus unde computabiles fuerint: et quod attornati illi ad profra et computationem hujusmodi

be holden from day to day in the Gildhall of the same town before the Mayor of that town, or his deputy, and the Sheriffs of the same town for the time being. And that the Mayor of that town for the time being, or his deputy, and the Sheriffs of that town for the time being shall have, from the said fifteenth day of the month of September, power and authority to hear and determine in that Court all manner of pleas, suits, plaints, causes and demands, and also actions real, personal, and mixed whatsoever, moved or to be moved within the same town and the liberty and precincts of the same town as they extend or are used, except as before-excepted, as well in the presence of us, our heirs and successors, as in the absence of us, our heirs and successors, together with all manner of profits of that Court henceforth in the future in any wise whatsoever happening or accruing, to be paid to the Sheriffs of the same town for the time being for their own proper use, without let or hindrance from us, our heirs or successors, or from the justices of us, our heirs or successors, whatsoever, or from the Steward or Marshall of the Household of us, our heirs or successors, or from the Escheators, Sheriffs, or other bailiffs or officers of us, our heirs or successors, whatsoever. And that the same Steward and Marshall shall not henceforth in the future in any wise intermeddle, nor shall any of them in any wise intermeddle with the cognizances of pleas of such contracts, covenants, trespasses, things, causes or matters whatsoever arising or happening within the same town or the liberty or precincts thereof as they extend or are used, except as before-excepted.

[margin: Henry VI. Its powers defined. The Burgesses to have all the profits of such Court. The Steward and Marshall of the King's Household not to interfere in the Borough.]

And that the said Escheator and Sheriffs of the same town of Nottingham for the time being may each year severally make their proffers and account before the Treasurer and Barons of the Exchequer of us, and of our heirs and successors, by the attornies of the same Escheator and Sheriffs of that town hereunto severally deputed and to be deputed by letters patent to be sealed under the seals of the offices of the same Escheator and Sheriffs of that town, of all manner of things touching the offices of Escheator and Sheriffs of the same town whereof they be accountable: and that those attornies shall be admitted by

[margin: The Escheator and Sheriffs may make their proffers and accounts at the Exchequer by attorneys.]

CHARTER OF HENRY VI. [1448

HENRY VI.

They shall not be compelled to attend in person to make their accounts.

facienda et reddenda loco ipsorum Escaëtoris et Vicecomitum per eosdem Thesaurarium et Barones juxta vim et effectum istarum nostrarum litterarum admittantur; absque hoc, quod dicti Escaëtor et Vicecomites ejusdem villae Notyngham', seu eorum successores, aut aliquis eorum, extra eandem villam ad computandum de aliquibus ad officia sua seu officium alicujus eorum spectantibus personaliter venire compellantur seu teneantur, aut eorum aliquis compellatur vel teneatur quovis modo:

The Escheator to take his oath within the Borough before the Coroners.

et quod quilibet Escaëtor illius villae Notyngham', qui pro tempore erit, statim post praefectionem suam, praestet singulis annis imperpetuum in eadem villa, et non alibi, sacramentum suum de officio illo bene et fideliter faciendo, coram Coronatoribus, vel uno Coronatorum, ejusdem villae pro tempore existentibus; absque eo, quod idem Escaëtor illius villae Notyngham', vel successores sui, ad sacramenta sua hujusmodi facienda extra eandem villam alibi coram aliquibus aliis seu aliquo alio venire compellatur seu compellantur: ita semper, quod infra duodecim dies proximo post electionem Majoris villae illius sequentes de nomine Escaëtoris illius villae singulis annis ad Scaccarium nostrum, heredum et successorum nostrorum, sub sigillo Majoratus ipsius villae Notyngham' certificetur.

The name of the Escheator to be returned into the Exchequer.

Grant of chattels of felons and outlaws;

Concessimus etiam, ex mero motu et certa scientia nostris praedictis, pro nobis, heredibus et successoribus nostris praedictis, praefatis nunc Burgensibus dictae villae Notyngham', et successoribus suis imperpetuum, catalla quarumcumque personarum tam ad sectam nostram, heredum vel successorum nostrorum, quam aliorum quorumcumque pro aliquibus feloniis, murdris, aut aliis offensis dampnatarum, convictarum aut aliquo modo attinctarum, ac aliarum personarum quarumcumque ex quacumque causa utlagatarum tam ad sectam nostram, heredum

of disavowed chattels of felones de se and of deodands;

vel successorum nostrorum, quam aliorum quorumcumque; necnon catalla disadvocata felonum de se, et deodanda infra eandem villam Notyngham' et procinctus ejusdem villae prout se extendunt vel utuntur, exceptis prae-exceptis, reperta et inventa.

of all amercements, ransoms, forfeited issues, and fines from the inhabitants of the borough;

Et quod iidem nunc Burgenses illius villae, et successores sui, habeant imperpetuum omnia amerciamenta, redemptiones, et exitus forisfactos et forisfaciendos, ac omnes fines pro transgressionibus et aliis delictis, negligentiis, mesprisionibus, et contemptibus quibuscumque; ac etiam fines pro licentia concordandi,

the same Treasurer and Barons to make and render such proffers and account in the stead of the said Escheator and Sheriffs according to the force and effect of these our letters; without the said Escheator and Sheriffs of the same town of Nottingham, or their successors, or any of them, being compelled or bound, or any of them in any wise being compelled or bound to personally come out of the same town to account for anything pertaining to their offices or the office of any of them: and that every Escheator of that town of Nottingham for the time being, immediately after his appointment, shall take his oath every year for ever in the same town, and not elsewhere, to well and faithfully execute that office, before the Coroners, or one of the Coroners, of the same town for the time being; without the same Escheator of that town of Nottingham, or his successors, being compelled to come to make such their oath out of the same town elsewhere before any one else: provided always, that within twelve days next following after the election of Mayor of that town it be certified, under the seal of the Mayoralty of that town of Nottingham, every year at the Exchequer of us, our heirs and successors, of the name of the Escheator of that town.

Henry VI.

They shall not be compelled to attend in person to make their accounts.

The Escheator to take his oath within the Borough before the Coroners.

The name of the Escheator to be returned into the Exchequer.

We have also granted, of our mere motion and certain knowledge aforesaid, for us, our heirs and successors aforesaid, to the aforesaid present Burgesses of the said town of Nottingham, and to their successors for ever, the chattels of all persons whatsoever condemned, convicted or in any wise attainted either at the suit of us, our heirs or successors, or of other persons whatsoever for any felonies, murders, or other offences, and of other persons whatsoever outlawed from whatsoever cause either at the suit of us, our heirs or successors, or of other persons whatsoever; and also the chattels disavowed of *felones de se*, and deodands discovered and found within the same town of Nottingham and the precincts of the same town as they extend or are used, except as before-excepted. And that the same present Burgesses of that town, and their successors, shall have for ever all amercements, ransoms, and issues forfeited and to be forfeited, and all fines for trespasses and other offences, negligences, misprisions, and contempts whatsoever; and also fines for licence to agree, and all things that may in any wise pertain to us and our

Grant of chattels of felons and outlaws;

of disavowed chattels of felones de se and of deodands;

of all amercements, ransoms, forfeited issues, and fines from the inhabitants of the borough;

Henry VI.

of all fines, etc., from the sureties of any person dwelling within the borough, in whatsoever royal court they may be forfeited.

et omnia, quae ad nos et heredes nostros quovis modo pertinere poterunt de hominibus vel aliquibus tenentibus vel habitantibus villae illius; necnon omnia exitus, fines, et amerciamenta de quibuscumque plegiis et manucaptoribus alicujus personae infra eandem villam Notyngham' commorantis, seu ibidem integre vel non integre tenentis existentis, licet persona illa seu plegii vel manucaptores illi de nobis, heredibus vel successoribus nostris, seu de aliis tenuerit, vel tenuerint, necnon de omnibus et singulis burgensibus ejusdem villae, tam residentibus quam non residentibus, licet illi integre tenentes ibidem non fuerint seu ibidem vel alibi de nobis, heredibus et successoribus nostris, seu de aliis tenuerint, in quibuscumque Curiis nostris, heredum vel successorum nostrorum, tam coram nobis, heredibus et successoribus nostris, ubicumque fuerimus, quam coram nobis, heredibus et successoribus nostris, in Cancellaria nostra, heredum vel successorum nostrorum, ac etiam coram Thesaurario et Baronibus nostris, heredum et successorum nostrorum, de Scaccario, et coram Justitiariis nostris, heredum et successorum nostrorum, de Banco, et coram Senescallo et Marescallo seu Clerico Mercati Hospitii nostri, heredum et successorum nostrorum, qui pro tempore fuerint, et in aliis Curiis nostris, heredum et successorum nostrorum, quibuscumque, et coram Justitiariis Itinerantibus ad Communia Placita seu ad Placita Forestae, et quibuscumque aliis Justitiariis et ministris nostris, heredum et successorum nostrorum, tam in praesentia nostra, heredum et successorum nostrorum, quam

The Burgesses shall have power to levy and receive all such fines, etc.

in absentia nostra, heredum et successorum nostrorum: et quod ipsi per se vel per ministros suos omnia fines, amerciamenta, redemptiones, exitus, forisfacturasque hujusmodi, et omnia, quae ad nos, heredes vel successores nostros, pertinere deberent, si praesens concessio nostra facta non fuisset, levare, percipere, et habere possint, sine occasione vel impedimento nostri, heredum vel successorum nostrorum, Justitiariorum, Escaëtorum, Vicecomitum, Coronatorum, aut aliorum ballivorum seu ministrorum nostrorum quorumcumque.

They may elect from themselves seven Aldermen;

Et ulterius, ex mero motu et certa scientia nostris praedictis, concessimus, pro nobis, heredibus et successoribus nostris praedictis, praefatis nunc Burgensibus dictae villae Notyngham', ac eorum heredibus et successoribus imperpetuum, quod iidem Burgenses, ac eorum heredes et successores, de tempore in

heirs from the men or any tenants or inhabitants of that town; HENRY VI. and also all issues, fines, and amercements from whatsoever pledges and mainpernors of any person dwelling within the same town of Nottingham, or being there wholly or not wholly a tenant, although that person or those pledges or mainpernors have holden of us, our heirs or successors, or of others, as well as from all and singular the burgesses of the same town, both resident and not resident, although they have not been wholly tenants there or have holden there or elsewhere of us, our heirs and successors, or of any others, in whatsoever the Courts of us, our heirs or successors, as well before us, our heirs and successors, wheresoever we may be, as before us, our heirs and successors, in the Chancery of us, our heirs or successors, and also before the Treasurer and Barons of us, our heirs and successors, of the Exchequer, and before the Justices of us, our heirs and successors, of the Bench, and before the Steward and Marshall or Clerk of the Market of the Household of us, our heirs and successors, for the time being, and in other the Courts of us, our heirs and successors, whatsoever, and before the Justices in Eyre for Common Pleas or for Pleas of the Forest, and whatsoever other Justices and officers of us, our heirs and successors, as well in the presence of us, our heirs and successors, as in the absence of us, our heirs and successors: and that they by themselves or by their officers may levy, receive, and have all such fines, amercements, ransoms, issues, and forfeitures, and all things that ought to pertain to us, our heirs or successors, if this our present grant had not been made, without let or hindrance from us, our heirs or successors, Justices, Escheators, Sheriffs, Coroners, or from other our bailiffs or officers whatsoever.

of all fines, etc., from the sureties of any person dwelling within the borough, in whatsoever royal court they may be forfeited.

The Burgesses shall have power to levy and receive all such fines, etc.

And furthermore, of our mere motion and certain knowledge aforesaid, we have granted, for us, our heirs and successors aforesaid, to the aforesaid present Burgesses of the said town of Nottingham, and to their heirs and successors for ever, that the same Burgesses, and their heirs and successors, may elect from

They may elect from themselves seven Aldermen;

HENRY VI.

of whom one shall always be elected Mayor.

The Aldermen are to hold office for life, unless they resign or be amoved for some notorious reason by the Mayor and Burgesses.

tempus eligere possint de se ipsis septem Aldermannos, quorum quidem Aldermannorum unus semper in Majorem villae illius eligatur ac Major ejusdem villae existat: qui quidem Aldermanni sic electi in hujusmodi officiis Aldermannorum ejusdem villae durante vita sua permaneant et existant, et quilibet eorum permaneat et existat, nisi ipsi, aut eorum aliquis, per suam specialem requisitionem residuis burgensibus villae illius pro tempore existentibus faciendam, seu propter aliquam notabilem causam ab Aldermanniis suis seu Aldermannia sua per Majorem et Burgenses villae illius pro tempore existentes ammoti fuerint, seu ammotus fuerit; et quod, obiente seu qualitercumque decedente vel ammoto hujusmodi Aldermanno ab officio suo Aldermanniae, habeant Major et Burgenses ejusdem villae pro tempore existentes, ac eorum heredes et successores imperpetuum, plenam potestatem et auctoritatem tenore praesentium eligendi unum alium burgensem de se ipsis in Aldermannum villae illius loco ipsius Aldermanni sic obientis, decedentis, vel ammoti, et sic de tempore in tempus imperpetuum obiente, decedente, vel ammoto aliquo hujusmodi Aldermanno villae illius in forma supra dicta.

The Aldermen to be Justices of the Peace within the Borough.

Et quod Aldermanni ejusdem villae pro tempore existentes sint Justitiarii nostri, heredum et successorum nostrorum, ad pacem infra eandem villam et libertatem et procinctus ejusdem villae prout se extendunt vel utuntur, exceptis prae-exceptis, conservandam imperpetuum; et quod septem Aldermanni illi, sex, quinque, quatuor et tres illorum (quorum Majorem villae illius pro tempore existentem unum praesentem esse volumus), plenam habeant potestatem et auctoritatem ad inquirenda, audienda et terminanda tam omnimodas felonias, murdra, transgressiones et mesprisiones, quam omnimoda alia causas, querelas, contemptus et malefacta, ac cetera quaecumque, quae ad aliquos Justitiarios Pacis infra regnum nostrum Angliae pertinent seu pertinere poterunt seu debebunt in futurum ad audiendum, inquirendum et terminandum, vel quovis modo corrigendum, infra eandem villam ac libertatem et procinctus ejusdem prout se extendunt vel utuntur, exceptis prae-exceptis, qualitercumque contingentia seu emergentia, necnon correctionem et punitionem eorundem, adeo plene et integre sicut Custodes Pacis et Justitiarii ad felonias, transgressiones et alia malefacta audienda [et] determinanda assignati et assignandi, ac Justitiarii Servient[i]um,

time to time from amongst themselves seven Aldermen, of which Aldermen one shall always be chosen Mayor of that town and shall be Mayor of the same town: which Aldermen so elected to such offices of Aldermen of the same town shall remain and be during their lifetime, and each of them shall remain and be, unless they, or any of them, be removed from their or his Aldermanship by their special request to be made to the rest of the burgesses of that town for the time being, or on account of any notable cause by the Mayor and Burgesses of that town for the time being; and that, when such Alderman die or in any wise depart or be removed from his office of Aldermanship, the Mayor and Burgesses of the same town for the time being, and their heirs and successors for ever, shall have full power and authority by the tenor of these presents to choose one other burgess from themselves as Alderman of that town in the stead of the Alderman so dying, departing, or removed, and so from time to time for ever when any such Alderman of that town die, depart or be removed in form abovesaid. And that the Aldermen of the same town for the time being shall be Justices of us, our heirs and successors, to keep the peace for ever within the same town and the liberty and precincts of the same town as they extend or are used, except as before-excepted; and that those seven Aldermen, six, five, four and three of them (of whom we will that the Mayor of that town for the time being shall be one present), shall have full power and authority to inquire, hear and determine as well all manner of felonies, murders, trespasses and misprisions as all manner of other causes, plaints, contempts and evil deeds, and other things whatsoever that do pertain or may or ought hereafter to pertain to any Justices of the Peace within our realm of England to hear, inquire and determine, or in any wise to correct, within the same town and the liberty and precincts of the same as they extend or are used, except as before-excepted, in any wise happening or arising, as well as the correction and punishment of the same, as fully and wholly as the Keepers of the Peace and Justices assigned and to be assigned to hear and determine felonies, trespasses and other evil deeds, and as Justices of Servants, Labourers and other Crafts have or shall have in any wise in the future in the County of Nottingham or

Henry VI. Of whom one shall always be elected Mayor.

The Aldermen are to hold office for life, unless they resign or be amoved for some notorious reason by the Mayor and Burgesses.

The Aldermen to be Justices of the Peace within the Borough.

E

Laboratorum et aliorum Artificiorum[1] in Comitatu Notyngham' seu alibi infra regnum nostrum Angliae extra villam et libertatem praedictas habent seu habebunt qualitercumque in futurum.

Grant of all fines arising from such Justiceship.

Concessimus insuper, ex mero motu et certa scientia nostris praedictis, pro nobis, heredibus et successoribus nostris praedictis, eisdem Burgensibus villae praedictae, ac heredibus et successoribus suis imperpetuum, quod ipsi imperpetuum habeant omnimoda fines, exitus forisfactos, et amerciamenta coram aliquibus Aldermannis et Majore ejusdem villae et Custodibus Pacis, seu ratione Justitiariae Pacis ibidem, facta vel fienda, forisfacta seu forisfienda, aut ratione hujusmodi Justitiariae Pacis ibidem infra eandem villam ac libertatem et procinctus ejusdem villae prout se extendunt vel utuntur, exceptis prae-exceptis, qualitercumque provenientia, per ministros suos proprios levanda et percipienda, in auxilium et supportationem grandium onerum eidem villae in dies incumbentium aut in eadem contingentium et emergentium.

Grant of forfeited victuals, etc.

Et quod praedicti nunc Burgenses ejusdem villae Notyngham', eorumque heredes et successores imperpetuum, habeant forisfacturam omnium victualium infra villam et procinctus illos per legem Angliae qualitercumque forisfiendarum; videlicet, panis, vini et cervisiae, ac aliorum victualium quorumcumque, quae ad mercandisas non pertinent.

Exemption from jurisdiction of the Steward and Marshal of the King's Household.

Et insuper, ex mero motu et certa scientia nostris praedictis, concessimus et per praesentes confirmamus, pro nobis, heredibus et successoribus nostris praedictis, praefatis nunc Burgensibus dictae villae Notyngham', ac eorum heredibus et successoribus praedictis imperpetuum, quod Senescallus et Marescallus Hospitii nostri, heredum vel successorum nostrorum, ac Clericus Mercati Hospitii nostri, heredum seu successorum nostrorum, de cetero nec in praesentia nostra, nec in absentia nostra, heredum vel successorum nostrorum, non ingrediantur nec sedeant, nec eorum aliquis ingrediatur nec sedeat, infra eandem villam aut libertatem et procinctus ejusdem villae prout se extendunt vel utuntur, exceptis prae-exceptis, ad officia sua seu officium alicujus eorum ibidem in aliquo excercenda seu quovis modo exequenda vel facienda, nec in placitum trahant, vel trahat, aliquos burgenses ejusdem villae aut aliquas personas infra eandem villam seu libertatem et procinctus ejusdem villae prout se extendunt vel utuntur, exceptis prae-exceptis, residentes pro

elsewhere within our realm of England outside the town and liberty aforesaid.

Grant of all fines arising from such justiceship.

We have moreover granted, of our mere motion and certain knowledge aforesaid, for us, our heirs and successors aforesaid, to the same Burgesses of the aforesaid town, and their heirs and successors for ever, that they shall have for ever all manner of fines, issues forfeited, and amercements made or to be made, forfeited or to be forfeited before any of the Aldermen and the Mayor of the same town and the Keepers of the Peace, or by reason of the Justiceship of the Peace there, or by reason of such Justiceship of the Peace there within the same town and the liberty and precincts of the same town as they extend or are used, except as before-excepted, in any wise arising, to be levied and received by their own officers, in aid and support of the great charges daily incumbent upon the same town or within the same happening and arising. And that the aforesaid present Burgesses of the same town of Nottingham, and their heirs and successors for ever, shall have the forfeiture of all victuals to be forfeited in any wise by the law of England within that town and those precincts; to wit, of bread, wine and ale, and of other victuals whatsoever that do not pertain to merchandise.

Grant of forfeited victuals, etc.

And furthermore, of our mere motion and certain knowledge aforesaid, we have granted and by these presents we do confirm, for us, our heirs and successors aforesaid, to the aforesaid present Burgesses of the said town of Nottingham, and to their heirs and successors aforesaid for ever, that the Steward and Marshall of the Household of us, our heirs or successors, and the Clerk of the Market of the Household of us, our heirs or successors, shall not henceforth, either in the presence or in the absence of us, our heirs or successors, enter or sit, nor shall any one of them enter or sit, within the same town or the liberty and precincts of the same town as they extend or are used, except as before-excepted, to exercise or in any wise execute or do their offices or the office of any one of them there in anything, nor shall they draw any burgesses of the same town or any persons resident within the same town or the liberty and precincts of the same town as they extend or are used, except as before-excepted, into pleas before them, or any of them, for any

Exemption from jurisdiction of the Steward and Marshal of the King's Household.

---

¹ So in MS. for *artificum*.

HENRY VI. aliquibus materiis, causis, placitis, querelis, aut rebus quibuscumque coram eis, seu eorum aliquo, contingentibus seu existentibus quoquo modo in futurum.

The Aldermen may wear gowns like the Mayor and Aldermen of London.

Concessimus etiam, ex mero motu et certa scientia nostris praedictis, et licentiam dedimus, pro nobis, heredibus et successoribus nostris praedictis, praefatis nunc Burgensibus praedictae villae Notyngham', et successoribus suis, ac cuicumque alii burgensi ejusdem villae pro tempore existenti, qui Aldermannus villae illius existet, quod Aldermanni ejusdem villae imperpetuum pro tempore existentes uti valeant togis, capiciis, et collobiis de una secta et una liberata, simul cum furruris et linaturis collobiis illis convenientibus,[1] eisdem modo et forma prout Major et Aldermanni Civitatis nostrae London' utuntur, Statuto de Liberatis Pannorum et Capiciorum aut aliquo alio Statuto sive ordinatione ante haec tempora editis non obstantibus.

The Escheators and Sheriffs to answer by attorney at the Exchequer for all things pertaining to the crown, excepting fines, etc., granted to the Burgesses.

Volumus tamen, quod quilibet praedictorum Escaëtorum et Vicecomitum villae illius pro tempore existentium, prout ad suum spectat officium, de omni eo infra eandem villam ac libertatem et procinctum ejusdem villae—exceptis omnimodis finibus, exitibus, et amerciamentis praedictis coram Justitiariis Pacis infra eandem villam et procinctus ejusdem villae prout se extendunt vel utuntur, exceptis prae-exceptis, seu ratione Justitiariae Pacis ibidem factis seu faciendis, forisfactis vel forisfiendis, qualitercumque provenientibus, et exceptis ceteris praemissis praefatis nunc Burgensibus villae illius, et successoribus suis, per nos virtute praesentium, ut praemittitur, concessis—quod ad nos et heredes et successores nostros de jure pertineret, et de quo Escaëtores et Vicecomites nostri dicti Comitatus Notyngham', seu eorum alter, coram Thesaurario et Baronibus de Scaccario nostro, heredum et successorum nostrorum, si praesens carta nostra cisdem nunc Burgensibus facta non existeret, computare deberent seu deberet, coram eisdem Thesaurario et Baronibus compotum suum per attornatos suos, ut praedictum est, reddere teneantur, ac nobis, et praefatis heredibus ac successoribus nostris, inde, prout justum fuerit, respondere teneantur.

The Mayor and Burgesses may enjoy all privileges, etc.,

Proviso semper, quod praedicti nunc Major et Burgenses dictae villae Notyngham', nec eorum successores, ad aliqua libertates, franchesias, seu privilegia Burgensibus villae illius, seu

matters, causes, pleas, plaints, or other things whatsoever happening or existing in any wise hereafter.

Henry VI.

We have also granted, of our mere motion and certain knowledge aforesaid, and have given licence, for us, our heirs and successors aforesaid, to the aforesaid present Burgesses of the aforesaid town of Nottingham, and to their successors, and to every other burgess of the same town for the time being who shall be an Alderman of that town, that the Aldermen of the same town for ever for the time being may use gowns, hoods, and cloaks of one suit and one livery, together with furs and linings suitable to those cloaks, in the same manner and form as the Mayor and Aldermen of our City of London do use, the Statute of Liveries of Cloths and of Hoods or any other Statute or ordinance heretofore issued notwithstanding.

The Aldermen may wear gowns like the Mayor and Aldermen of London.

We do nevertheless will, that each of the aforesaid Escheators and Sheriffs of that town for the time being shall be bound, as pertains to their office, to render by their attorneys, as is aforesaid, their account of everything that ought of right to pertain to us and our heirs and successors within the same town and the liberty and precincts of the same town, and whereof our Escheators and Sheriffs of the said County of Nottingham, or either of them, ought to account before the Treasurer and Barons of the Exchequer of us, our heirs and successors, if our present charter had not been made to the same present Burgesses,—excepting all manner of fines, issues, and amercements aforesaid made or to be made, forfeited or to be forfeited, in any wise accruing before the Justices of the Peace within the same town and the precincts of the same town as they extend or are used, except as before-excepted, or by reason of the Justiceship of the Peace there, and excepting the other premises granted by us to the aforesaid present Burgesses of that town, and to their successors, by virtue of these presents, as is aforesaid,—before the same Treasurer and Barons, and shall be bound to answer therefore to us, and to our aforesaid heirs and successors, as right shall require.

The Escheators and Sheriffs to answer by attorney at the Exchequer for all things pertaining to the crown, excepting fines, etc., granted to the Burgesses.

Provided always, that the aforesaid present Mayor and Burgesses of the said town of Nottingham, or their successors, shall not be excluded, barred or stopped in any wise by the acceptance

The Mayor and Burgesses may enjoy all privileges, etc.,

---

¹ *convenientibus,*] '*convenienientibus,*' MS.

<small>HENRY VI.</small>

<small>that pertained to the Bailiffs and Burgesses.</small>

Ballivis et Burgensibus ejusdem villae per antea quovis modo spectantia seu pertinentia, licet eadem libertates, franchesiae seu privilegia, aut eorum aliquod, per praesentes dictis nunc Burgensibus villae illius et successoribus suis concedantur vel concedatur, quoquo modo clamanda et habenda in jure et titulo suis sibi per antea pertinentibus seu spectantibus, aliquo modo per acceptationem praesentium excludantur, barrentur aut estoppentur; set quod bene licebit dicti nunc Majori et Burgensibus ejusdem villae et successoribus suis omnia et singula hujusmodi libertates, franchesias et privilegia Burgensibus villae illius aut Ballivis et Burgensibus villae illius per antea pertinentia vel de jure pertinere debentia in jure et titulo suis sibi inde ante datam praesentium pertinentibus vel spectantibus clamare, gaudere et habere, aliqua concessione de aliquo eorundem libertatum, franchesiarum seu privilegiorum in praesentibus facta seu acceptatione praesentium per eosdem Majorem et Burgenses vel successores suos non obstante.

<small>Enactment clause.</small>

Quare volumus et firmiter praecipimus, pro nobis, heredibus et successoribus nostris praedictis, quod praefati Burgenses villae nostrae praedictae, ac eorum heredes et successores, omnia et singula hujusmodi cognitiones, franchesias, libertates, et immunitates, ac omnia alia praemissa, prout superius specialiter expressantur, habeant, teneant et excerceant, ac eis, et eorum singulis, plene, libere, integre, pacifice et quiete imperpetuum gaudeant et utantur, absque impetitione, perturbatione, molestatione, seu impedimento nostri, heredum vel successorum nostrorum, aut aliquorum officiariorum seu ministrorum nostrorum, heredum vel successorum nostrorum quorumcumque, sicut praedictum est, modo et forma superius declaratis, aliquo dono sive concessione per nos aut per aliquem progenitorum nostrorum Burgensibus ejusdem villae Notyngham' vel praedecessoribus suis ante haec tempora factis, et quod inde seu de valore catallorum, amerciamentorum, exituum, finium, seu ceterorum praemissorum expressa mentio facta non existit, non obstante.

In cujus, etc. Teste Rege, apud Wynton', xxviij. die Junii.
Per Breve de Privato Sigillo, et pro quinque marcis solutis in Hanaperio.   Rot. Litt. Pat., 27 Hen. VI., pars II. m. 6.

of these presents from claiming and having, in their right and title heretofore pertaining or belonging to them, any liberties, franchises or privileges heretofore in any wise belonging or pertaining to the Burgesses of that town, or to the Bailiffs and Burgesses of the same town, although the same liberties, franchises or privileges, or any of them, be not granted by these presents to the said present Burgesses of that town and their successors; but that it shall be lawful to the said present Mayor and Burgesses of the same town and their successors to claim, enjoy and have all and singular such liberties, franchises and privileges heretofore pertaining or that ought of right to pertain to the Burgesses of that town or to the Bailiffs and Burgesses of that town in their right and title thereunto to them pertaining or belonging before the date of these presents, notwithstanding any grant of any of the same liberties, franchises or privileges made in these presents, and notwithstanding the acceptance of these presents by the same Mayor and Burgesses or their successors.

HENRY VI.

that pertained to the Bailiffs and Burgesses.

Wherefore we will and firmly enjoin, for us, our heirs and successors aforesaid, that the aforesaid Burgesses of our town aforesaid, and their heirs and successors, shall have, hold and exercise all and singular such cognizances, franchises, liberties, immunities, and all the other premises, as they are above specifically expressed, and that they shall enjoy and use them and each of them fully, freely, wholly, peacefully and quietly for ever, without impeachment, perturbation, molestation or let from us, our heirs or successors, or of any officers or ministers of us, our heirs or successors whomsoever, as is aforesaid, in the manner and form above declared, notwithstanding any gift or grant heretofore made by us or by any of our progenitors to the Burgesses of the same town of Nottingham or to their predecessors, and notwithstanding that express mention has not been made thereof or of the value of the chattels, amercements, issues, fines, or other the premises.

Enactment clause.

In witness, etc. Witness the King, at Winchester, the 28th day of June.

By Writ of Privy Seal, and for five marks paid into the Hanaper. Patent Roll, 27 Hen. VI., part II. m. 6.

XVI.—*Charter of King Edward IV.*
1462, May 1.

EDWARD IV.   REX omnibus, ad quos, etc., salutem. Inspeximus litteras patentes Henrici Sexti, nuper de facto et non de jure Regis Angliae, factas in hacc verba: 'HENRICUS, Dei gratia' [*etc., reciting Charter of King Henry VI., No. XV.*].

Confirmation of preceding charters.   Nos autem, omnia et singula franchesias, libertates, privilegia, quietantias, immunitates, concessiones, confirmationes et restitutiones praedicta rata habentes et grata, ea, pro nobis, heredibus et successoribus nostris, quantum in nobis est, acceptamus, approbamus [et] ratificamus, ac omnia et singula franchesias, libertates, privilegia, quietantias [et] immunitates praedicta dilectis nobis nunc Majori, Vicecomitibus et Burgensibus villae praedictae, ac Majori et Burgensibus ejusdem villae, heredibus et successoribus suis, tenore praesentium, concedimus et confirmamus, sicut cartae praedictae rationabiliter testantur, et prout iidem Major, Vicecomites et Burgenses ejusdem villae Notyngham', vel praedecessores sui, Majores, Vicecomites [et] Burgenses villae praedictae, aut Majores, Ballivi et Burgenses villae illius, unquam franchesiis, libertatibus, privilegiis, quietantiis et immunitatibus praedictis uti et gaudere debent, potuerunt, seu debuerunt, ipsique et praedecessores sui franchesiis, libertatibus, privilegiis, quietantiis, [et] immunitatibus illis unquam post confectionem cartarum praedictarum rationabiliter uti et gaudere consueverunt, potuerunt, vel debuerunt.

In cujus, etc. Teste Rege, apud Westmonasterium, primo die Maii.   Pro duabus marcis solutis in Hanaperio.
Rot. Litt. Pat., 2 Ed. IV., pars IV., m. 18.

XVII.—*Charter of King Henry VII.*
1505, June 4.

HENRY VII.   [1][H]ENRICUS, Dei gratia, [R]ex [A]ngliae et [F]ranciae et [D]ominus [H]iberniae, [o]mnibus, ad quos praesentes litterae pervenerint, salutem. [I]nspeximus litteras patentes Domini E[dwardi], nuper Regis Angliae Quarti, de confirmatione factas

---

[1] The letters here enclosed in brackets do not appear in the original. It was intended to illuminate these initials, blank spaces being left for their insertion by the

XVI.—*Charter of King Edward IV.*
1462, May 1.

THE KING to all to whom, etc., greeting. We have seen the letters patent of Henry the Sixth, late in deed but not of right King of England, made in these words: 'HENRY, by the grace of God' [*etc., reciting Charter of King Henry VI., No. XV.*].

We also, considering all and singular the franchises, liberties, privileges, acquittances, immunities, concessions, confirmations and restitutions aforesaid as valid and acceptable, do accept, approve [and] ratify them for us, our heirs and successors, so far as in us lies, and do grant and confirm, by the tenor of these presents, all and singular the franchises, liberties, privileges, acquittances [and] immunities aforesaid to our well-beloved the present Mayor, Sheriffs and Burgesses of the town aforesaid and to the Mayor and Burgesses of the same town, their heirs and successors, as the charters aforesaid do reasonably bear witness, and as the same Mayor, Sheriffs and Burgesses of the same town of Nottingham, or their predecessors, Mayors, Sheriffs [and] Burgesses of the town aforesaid, or Mayors, Bailiffs and Burgesses of that town, ought to, might have, or should have used and enjoyed at any time the franchises, liberties, privileges, acquittances, and immunities aforesaid, and as they or their predecessors have been wont, or might have, or should have reasonably used and enjoyed those franchises, liberties, privileges, acquittances, [and] immunities at any time after the making of the charters aforesaid.

In witness, etc. Witness the King, at Westminster, the first day of May. For two marks paid into the Hanaper.

Patent Roll, 2 Ed. IV., part IV., m. 18.

margin: EDWARD IV. Confirmation of preceding charters.

XVII.—*Charter of King Henry VII.*
1505, June 4.

HENRY, by the grace of God, King of England and France and Lord of Ireland, to all to whom these present letters shall come, greeting. We have inspected the letters patent of the Lord Edward the Fourth, late King of England, of confirmation

margin: HENRY VII.

---

illuminator. Charters, etc., are often met with in this incomplete state, they having been issued before the initials had been inserted.

Henry VII. in haec verba: 'EDWARDUS, Dei gratia, Rex Angliae et Franciae et Dominus Hiberniae, omnibus ad quos' [*etc., reciting Charter of King Edward IV., No. XVI.*].

Confirmation of preceding charters. Nos autem, litteras praedictas, necnon omnia et singula franchesias, libertates, privilegia, quietantias, immunitates, concessiones, confirmationes et restitutiones praedicta rata habentes et grata, ea, pro nobis, heredibus et successoribus nostris, quantum in nobis est, acceptamus, approbamus et ratificamus, ac omnia et singula franchesias, libertates, privilegia, quietantias et immunitates praedicta dilectis nobis nunc Majori, Vicecomitibus et Burgensibus villae praedictae ac Majori et Burgensibus ejusdem villae, heredibus et successoribus suis, tenore praesentium, concedimus et confirmamus, sicut cartae et litterae praedictae rationabiliter testantur, et prout iidem Major, Vicecomites et Burgenses ejusdem villae Notyngham', vel praedecessores sui, Majores, Vicecomites et Burgenses villae praedictae, aut Majores, Ballivi et Burgenses villae illius, unquam franchesiis, libertatibus, privilegiis, quietantiis et immunitatibus praedictis uti et gaudere debent, potuerunt, seu debuerunt, ipsique et praedecessores sui franchesiis, libertatibus, privilegiis, quietantiis, immunitatibus illis unquam post confectionem cartarum et litterarum praedictarum rationabiliter uti et gaudere consueverunt, potuerunt, vel debuerunt.

In cujus rei testimonium has litteras nostras fieri fecimus patentes. Teste me ipso apud Westmonasterium, quarto die Junii, anno regni nostri vicesimo.

Pro triginta et tribus solidis et quatuor denariis solutis in Hanaperio. Hatton.

4175.

XVIII.—*Charter of King Henry VIII.*
1510, November 11.

Henry VIII. [1]HENRICUS, Dei gratia, Rex Angliae et Franciae et Dominus Hiberniae, omnibus, ad quos praesentes litterae pervenerint, salutem. Inspeximus litteras patentes Domini Henrici, nuper Regis Angliae Septimi, patris nostri, de confirmatione factas in haec verba: 'HENRICUS, Dei gratia' [*etc., reciting Charter of King Henry VII., No. XVII.*].

[1] This is taken from the recital in the Charter of Philip and Mary (No. 4177).

made in these words: 'EDWARD, by the grace of God, King of England and France and Lord of Ireland, to all to whom' [*etc.*, *reciting Charter of King Edward IV., No. XVI.*]. _{HENRY VII.}

We also, considering the letters aforesaid, as well as all and singular the franchises, liberties, privileges, acquittances, immunities, concessions, confirmations and restitutions aforesaid as valid and acceptable, do accept, approve and ratify them for us, our heirs and successors, so far as in us lies, and do grant and confirm, by the tenor of these presents, all and singular the franchises, liberties, privileges, acquittances and immunities aforesaid to our well-beloved the present Mayor, Sheriffs and Burgesses of the town aforesaid and to the Mayor and Burgesses of the same town, their heirs and successors, as the charters and letters aforesaid do reasonably bear witness, and as the same Mayor, Sheriffs and Burgesses of the same town of Nottingham, or their predecessors, Mayors, Sheriffs and Burgesses of the town aforesaid, or Mayors, Bailiffs and Burgesses of that town, ought to, might have, or should have used and enjoyed at any time the franchises, liberties, privileges, acquittances and immunities aforesaid, and as they and their predecessors have been wont, or might have, or should have reasonably used and enjoyed those franchises, liberties, privileges, acquittances, immunities at any time after the making of the charters and letters aforesaid. [Confirmation of preceding charters.]

In witness whereof we have caused these our letters to be made patent. Witness myself at Westminster, the fourth day of June, in the twentieth year of our reign.

For three and thirty shillings and fourpence
paid into the Hanaper. Hatton.
4175.

XVIII.—*Charter of King Henry VIII.*
1510, November 11.

¹ HENRY, by the grace of God, King of England and France and Lord of Ireland, to all to whom the present letters shall come, greeting. We have inspected the letters patent of the Lord Henry the Seventh, late King of England, our father, of confirmation made in these words: 'HENRY, by the grace of God' [*etc., reciting Charter of King Henry VII., No. XVII.*]. [Henry VIII.]

HENRY VIII.

Confirmation of preceding charters.

Nos autem, litteras praedictas, necnon omnia et singula franchesias, libertates, privilegia, quietantias, immunitates, concessiones, confirmationes et restitutiones praedicta rata habentes et grata, ea, pro nobis, heredibus et successoribus nostris, quantum in nobis est, acceptamus, approbamus et ratificamus, ac omnia et singula franchesias, libertates, privilegia, quietantias et immunitates praedicta dilectis nobis nunc Majori, Vicecomitibus et Burgensibus villae praedictae ac Majori et Burgensibus ejusdem villae, heredibus et successoribus suis, tenore praesentium, concedimus et confirmamus, sicut cartae et litterae praedictae rationabiliter testantur, et prout iidem Major, Vicecomites et Burgenses ejusdem villae Notyngham', vel praedecessores sui, Majores, Vicecomites et Burgenses villae praedictae, aut Majores, Ballivi et Burgenses villae illius, unquam franchesiis, libertatibus, privilegiis, quietantiis et immunitatibus praedictis uti et gaudere debent, potuerunt, seu debuerunt, ipsique et praedecessores sui franchesiis, libertatibus, privilegiis, quietantiis, immunitatibus illis unquam post confectionem cartarum et litterarum praedictarum rationabiliter uti et gaudere consueverunt, potuerunt vel debuerunt.

In cujus rei testimonium has litteras nostras fieri fecimus patentes. Teste me ipso apud Westmonasterium, undecimo die Novembris, anno regni nostri secundo.

XIX.—*Charter of King Edward VI.*
1548-9, March 7.

EDWARD VI.

[1]EDWARDUS Sextus, Dei gratia, Angliae, Franciae et Hiberniae Rex, Fidei Defensor, et in terra Ecclesiae Anglicanae et Hibernicae Supremum Caput, omnibus, ad quos praesentes litterae pervenerint, salutem. Inspeximus litteras patentes celebris memoriae Domini Henrici, nuper Regis Angliae, Octavi, patris nostri praecharissimi, de confirmatione factas in haec verba : 'HENRICUS, Dei gratia' [*etc., reciting Charter of Henry VIII., No. XVIII.*].

Confirmation of preceding charters.

Nos autem, litteras praedictas, necnon omnia et singula franchesias, libertates, privilegia, quietantias, immunitates, concessiones, confirmationes et restitutiones praedicta rata habentes

[1] Taken from the recital in the Charter of Philip and Mary (No. XX.).

We also, considering the letters aforesaid, as well as all and *Henry VIII.* singular the franchises, liberties, privileges, acquittances, immunities, concessions, confirmations and restitutions aforesaid as valid *Confirmation of preceding charters.* and acceptable, do accept, approve and ratify them for us, our heirs and successors, so far as in us lies, and do grant and confirm, by the tenor of these presents, all and singular the franchises, liberties, privileges, acquittances and immunities aforesaid to our well-beloved the present Mayor, Sheriffs and Burgesses of the town aforesaid and to the Mayor and Burgesses of the same town, their heirs and successors, as the charters and letters aforesaid do reasonably bear witness, and as the same Mayor, Sheriffs and Burgesses of the same town of Nottingham, or their predecessors, Mayors, Sheriffs and Burgesses of the town aforesaid, or Mayors, Bailiffs and Burgesses of that town, ought to, might have, or should have used and enjoyed at any time the franchises, liberties, privileges, acquittances and immunities aforesaid, and as they and their predecessors have been wont, or might have, or should have reasonably used and enjoyed those franchises, liberties, privileges, acquittances, immunities at any time after the making of the charters and letters aforesaid.

In witness whereof we have caused these our letters to be made patent. Witness myself at Westminster, the eleventh day of November, in the second year of our reign.

XIX.—*Charter of King Edward VI.*

1548-9, March 7.

¹EDWARD the Sixth, by the grace of God, of England, *Edward VI.* France and Ireland King, Defender of the Faith, and upon earth the Supreme Head of the Church of England and Ireland, to all to whom these present letters shall come, greeting. We have inspected the letters patent of the Lord Henry the Eighth of renowned memory, late King of England, our full dear father, of confirmation made in these words: 'HENRY, by the grace of God' [*etc., reciting Charter of Henry VIII., No. XVIII.*].

We also, considering the letters aforesaid, as well as all and *Confirmation of preceding charters.* singular the franchises, liberties, privileges, acquittances, immunities, concessions, confirmations and restitutions aforesaid as valid

EDWARD VI. et grata, ea, pro nobis, heredibus et successoribus nostris, quantum in nobis est, acceptamus, approbamus et ratificamus, ac omnia et singula franchesias, libertates, privilegia, quietantias et immunitates praedicta dilectis nobis nunc Majori, Vicecomitibus et Burgensibus villae praedictae ac Majori et Burgensibus ejusdem villae, heredibus et successoribus suis, tenore praesentium, concedimus et confirmamus, sicut cartae et litterae praedictae rationabiliter testantur, et prout iidem Major, Vicecomites et Burgenses ejusdem villae Notyngham', vel praedecessores sui, Majores, Vicecomites et Burgenses villae praedictae, aut Majores, Ballivi et Burgenses villae illius, unquam franchesiis, libertatibus, privilegiis, quietantiis et immunitatibus praedictis uti et gaudere debent, potuerunt, seu debuerunt, ipsique et praedecessores sui franchesiis, libertatibus, privilegiis, quietantiis, immunitatibus illis unquam post confectionem cartarum et litterarum praedictarum rationabiliter uti et gaudere consueverunt, potuerunt, vel debuerunt.

In cujus rei testimonium has litteras nostras fieri fecimus patentes. Teste me ipso apud Westmonasterium, septimo die Martii, anno regni nostri tertio.

XX.—*Charter of Philip and Mary.*

1555, November 27.

PHILIP and MARY.

PHILIPPUS et MARIA, Dei gratia, Rex et Regina Angliae, Franciae, Neapolis, Jerusalem, et Hiberniae, Fidei Defensores, Principes Hispaniarum et Siciliae, Archiduces Austriae, Duces Mediolani, Burgundiae, et Brabantiae, Comites Haspurgi, Flandriae, et Tirolis, omnibus, ad quos praesentes litterae pervenerint, salutem. Inspeximus litteras patentes celebris memoriae Domini Edwardi, nuper Regis Angliae, Sexti, fratris nostri praecharissimi, de confirmatione factas in haec verba: 'EDWARDUS Sextus, Dei gratia' [*etc., reciting Charter of Edward VI., No. XIX.*].

Confirmation of preceding charters.

Nos autem, litteras praedictas, necnon omnia et singula franchesias, libertates, privilegia, quietantias, immunitates, concessiones, confirmationes et restitutiones praedicta rata habentes et grata, ea pro nobis, heredibus et successoribus nostris, quantum in nobis est, acceptamus, approbamus et ratificamus, ac

and acceptable, do accept, approve and ratify them for us, our heirs and successors, so far as in us lies, and do grant and confirm, by the tenor of these presents, all and singular the franchises, liberties, privileges, acquittances and immunities aforesaid to our well-beloved the present Mayor, Sheriffs and Burgesses of the town aforesaid and to the Mayor and Burgesses of the same town, their heirs and successors, as the charters and letters aforesaid do reasonably bear witness, and as the same Mayor, Sheriffs and Burgesses of the same town of Nottingham, or their predecessors, Mayors, Sheriffs and Burgesses of the town aforesaid, or Mayors, Bailiffs and Burgesses of that town, ought to, might have, or should have used and enjoyed at any time the franchises, liberties, privileges, acquittances and immunities aforesaid, and as they and their predecessors have been wont, or might have, or should have reasonably used and enjoyed those franchises, liberties, privileges, acquittances, immunities at any time after the making of the charters and letters aforesaid.

In witness whereof we have caused these our letters to be made patent. Witness myself at Westminster, the seventh day of March, in the third year of our reign.

[margin: EDWARD VI.]

XX.—*Charter of Philip and Mary.*

1555, November 27.

PHILIP and MARY, by the grace of God, King and Queen of England, France, Naples, Jerusalem, and Ireland, Defenders of the Faith, Princes of Spain and Sicily, Archdukes of Austria, Dukes of Milan, Burgundy, and Brabant, Counts of Hapsburg, Flanders, and Tyrol, to all to whom these present letters shall come, greeting. We have inspected the letters patent of the Lord Edward the Sixth of renowned memory, late King of England, our full dear brother, of confirmation made in these words: 'EDWARD the Sixth, by the grace of God' [*etc., reciting Charter of Edward VI., No. XIX.*].

[margin: PHILIP and MARY.]

We also, considering the letters aforesaid, as well as all and singular the franchises, liberties, privileges, acquittances, immunities, concessions, confirmations and restitutions aforesaid as valid and acceptable, do accept, approve and ratify them for us, our heirs and successors, so far as in us lies, and do grant and

[margin: Confirmation of preceding charters.]

PHILIP AND MARY. and omnia et singula franchesias, libertates, privilegia, quietantias et immunitates praedicta dilectis nobis nunc Majori, Vicecomitibus et Burgensibus villae praedictae ac Majori et Burgensibus ejusdem villae, heredibus et successoribus suis, tenore praesentium, concedimus et confirmamus, sicut cartae et litterae praedictae rationabiliter testantur, et prout iidem Major, Vicecomites et Burgenses ejusdem villae Notyngham', vel praedecessores sui, Majores, Vicecomites et Burgenses villae praedictae, aut Majores, Ballivi [et] Burgenses villae illius, unquam franchesiis, libertatibus, privilegiis, quietantiis et immunitatibus praedictis uti et gaudere debent, potuerunt, seu debuerunt, ipsique et praedecessores sui franchesiis, libertatibus, privilegiis, quietantiis, immunitatibus illis unquam post confectionem cartarum et litterarum praedictarum rationabiliter uti et gaudere consueverunt, potuerunt, vel debuerunt.

In cujus rei testimonium has litteras nostras fieri fecimus patentes. Testibus nobis ipsis, apud Westmonasterium, vicesimo septimo die Novembris, annis regnorum nostrorum secundo et tertio.   Hare.

4177.

XXI.—*Charter of Queen Elizabeth.*
1559-60, February 7.

ELIZABETH.   ELIZABETH, Dei gratia, Angliae, Franciae, et Hiberniae Regina, Fidei Defensor, etc., omnibus, ad quos praesentes litterae pervenerint, salutem. Inspeximus litteras patentes Domini Philippi Regis et Dominae Mariae, nuper Reginae Angliae, praecharissimae sororis nostrae, de confirmatione factas in haec verba: 'PHILIPPUS et MARIA, Dei gratia' [*etc., reciting Charter of Philip and Mary, No. XX.*].

Confirmation of preceding charters. Nos autem, litteras praedictas, necnon omnia et singula franchesias, libertates, privilegia, quietantias, immunitates, concessiones, confirmationes et restitutiones praedicta rata habentes et grata, ea, pro nobis, heredibus et successoribus nostris, quantum in nobis est, acceptamus, approbamus et ratificamus, ac omnia et singula franchesias, libertates, privilegia, quietantias et immunitates praedicta dilectis nobis nunc Majori, Vicecomitibus et Burgensibus villae praedictae ac Majori et Burgensibus ejusdem villae, heredibus et successoribus suis, tenore praesentium,

confirm, by the tenor of these presents, all and singular the franchises, liberties, privileges, acquittances and immunities aforesaid to our well-beloved the present Mayor, Sheriffs and Burgesses of the town aforesaid and to the Mayor and Burgesses of the same town, their heirs and successors, as the charters and letters aforesaid do reasonably bear witness, and as the same Mayor, Sheriffs and Burgesses of the same town of Nottingham, or their predecessors, Mayors, Sheriffs and Burgesses of the town aforesaid, or Mayors, Bailiffs [and] Burgesses of that town, ought to, might have, or should have used and enjoyed at any time the franchises, liberties, privileges, acquittances and immunities aforesaid, and as they and their predecessors have been wont, or might have, or should have reasonably used and enjoyed those franchises, liberties, privileges, acquittances, immunities at any time after the making of the charters and letters aforesaid. PHILIP and MARY.

In witness whereof we have caused these our letters to be made patent. Witness ourselves, at Westminster, the twenty-seventh day of November, in the second and third years of our reign.   Hare.

4177.

XXI.—*Charter of Queen Elizabeth.*
1559-60, February 7.

ELIZABETH, by the grace of God, of England, France, and Ireland Queen, Defender of the Faith, etc., to all to whom these present letters shall come, greeting. We have inspected the letters patent of the Lord King Philip and the Lady Mary, late Queen of England, our full dear sister, of confirmation made in these words: 'PHILIP and MARY, by the grace of God' [*etc., reciting Charter of Philip and Mary, No. XX.*]. ELIZABETH.

We also, considering the letters aforesaid, as well as all and singular the franchises, liberties, privileges, acquittances, immunities, concessions, confirmations and restitutions aforesaid as valid and acceptable, do accept, approve and ratify them for us, our heirs and successors, so far as in us lies, and do grant and confirm, by the tenor of these presents, all and singular the franchises, liberties, privileges, acquittances and immunities aforesaid to our well-beloved the present Mayor, Sheriffs and Burgesses of the town aforesaid and to the Mayor and Burgesses Confirmation of preceding charters.

F

ELIZABETH. concedimus et confirmamus, sicut cartae et litterae praedictae rationabiliter testantur, et prout iidem Major, Vicecomites et Burgenses ejusdem villae Notyngham', vel praedecessores sui, Majores, Vicecomites et Burgenses villae praedictae, aut Majores, Ballivi [et] Burgenses villae illius, unquam franchesiis, libertatibus, privilegiis, quietantiis et immunitatibus praedictis uti et gaudere debent, potuerunt, seu debuerunt, ipsique et praedecessores sui franchesiis, libertatibus, privilegiis, quietantiis, immunitatibus illis unquam post confectionem cartarum et litterarum praedictarum rationabiliter uti et gaudere consueverunt, potuerunt, vel debuerunt.

In cujus rei testimonium has litteras nostras fieri fecimus patentes. Teste me ipsa, apud Westmonasterium, septimo die Februarii, anno regni nostri secundo.[1]   Cordell'.   4178.

XXII.—*Charter of King James I.*
1604, April 11.

JAMES I. JACOBUS, Dei gratia, Angliae, Scotiae, Franciae, et Hiberniae Rex, Fidei Defensor, etc., omnibus, ad quos praesentes litterae pervenerint, salutem. Inspeximus literas patentes praecharissimae sororis nostrae Dominae Elizabeth, nuper Reginae Angliae, de confirmatione factas in haec verba: 'ELIZABETH, Dei gratia' [*etc., reciting Charter of Queen Elizabeth, No. XXI.*].

Confirmation of previous charters. Nos autem, cartas et literas praedictas ac omnia et singula in eisdem contenta et specificata rata habentes et grata, ea, pro nobis, heredibus et successoribus nostris, quantum in nobis est, acceptamus et approbamus, ac dilectis nobis nunc Majori, Vicecomitibus, et Burgensibus praedictae villae de Nottingham et Majori et Burgensibus ejusdem villae, heredibus et successoribus suis, tenore praesentium ratificamus et confirmamus, sicut cartae et literae praedictae in se rationabiliter testantur.

In cujus rei testimonium has literas nostras fieri fecimus patentes. Teste me ipso apud Westmonasterium, undecimo die Aprilis, anno regni nostri Angliae, Franciae, et Hiberniae secundo et Scotiae tricesimo septimo.[2]   T. Ravenscrofte.   4179.

[1] There is a contemporary note at the foot of the charter: 'Taxatur finis ad iiij. li.'=the fine (for passing the Charter) is taxed at £4.

[2] The following note occurs at the foot of the Charter: 'Finis taxatur ad vj. li. xiijs. iiijd. T. Ellesmere, Canc[ellarius]' = the Fine is taxed at £6 13s. 4d. T. Ellesmere, Chancellor.

of the same town, their heirs and successors, as the charters and ELIZABETH. letters aforesaid do reasonably bear witness, and as the same Mayor, Sheriffs and Burgesses of the same town of Nottingham, or their predecessors, Mayors, Sheriffs and Burgesses of the town aforesaid, or Mayors, Bailiffs [and] Burgesses of that town, ought to, might have, or should have used and enjoyed at any time the franchises, liberties, privileges, acquittances and immunities aforesaid, and as they and their predecessors have been wont, or might have, or should have reasonably used and enjoyed those franchises, liberties, privileges, acquittances, immunities at any time after the making of the charters and letters aforesaid.

In witness whereof we have caused these our letters to be made patent. Witness myself, at Westminster, the seventh day of February, in the second year of our reign.[1] Cordell. 4178.

XXII.—*Charter of King James I.*
1604, April 11.

JAMES, by the grace of God, of England, Scotland, France, JAMES I. and Ireland, King, Defender of the Faith, etc., to all to whom these present letters shall come, greeting. We have inspected the letters patent of our full dear sister Lady Elizabeth, late Queen of England, of confirmation made in these words: 'ELIZABETH, by the grace of God' [*etc., reciting Charter of Queen Elizabeth, No. XXI.*].

We also, esteeming the charters and letters aforesaid and all Confirmation and singular the things in the same contained and specified as charters. valid and acceptable, do, for us, our heirs and successors, so far as in us lies accept and approve them, and do ratify and confirm them by the tenor of these presents to our well-beloved the present Mayor, Sheriffs, and Burgesses of the aforesaid town of Nottingham and to the Mayor and Burgesses of the same town, their heirs and successors, as the charters and letters aforesaid in themselves do reasonably bear witness.

In witness whereof we have caused these our letters to be made patent. Witness myself at Westminster, the eleventh day of April, in the second year of our reign in England, France, and Ireland, and the thirty-seventh in Scotland.[2]

T. Ravenscroft. 4179.

XXIII.—*Exemplification of Charter of Henry VI. by King James I.*

1622-3, February 12.

JAMES I.

JACOBUS, Dei gratia, Angliae, Scotiae, Franciae, et Hiberniae Rex, Fidei Defensor, omnibus, ad quos praesentes literae pervenerint, salutem.

Inspeximus of Charter of Henry VI.

Inspeximus quasdam literas patentes Domini Henrici, nuper Regis Angliae, Sexti Majori, Ballivis, et Burgensibus villae de Notyngham factas, datas vicesimo octavo die Junii, anno regni sui vicesimo septimo, in Memorandis Scaccarii Thesaurarii nostri in dicto Scaccario nostro remanentibus et existentibus in haec verba, scilicet: 'REX, omnibus ad quos, etc.' [*reciting Charter of King Henry VI., No. XV.*].

Nos autem praemissa omnia et singula ad requisitionem et instantiam nunc Majoris et Burgensium dictae villae nostrae Notyngham sub sigillo Scaccarii nostri tenore praesentium duximus exemplificanda.

In cujus rei testimonium has litteras nostras fieri fecimus patentes. Teste praedilecto et fideli consanguineo et Commissario nostro Lionello, Comite Middlesexiae, Summo Thesaurario nostro Angliae, apud Westmonasterium, duodecimo die Februarii, anno regni nostri Angliae, Franciae, et Hiberniae vicesimo, et Scotiae quinquagesimo sexto.

XXIV.—*Charter of King Charles I.*

1626, December 8.

CHARLES I.

CAROLUS, Dei gratia, Angliae, Scotiae, Franciae, et Hiberniae Rex, Fidei Defensor, etc., omnibus, ad quos praesentes litterae pervenerint, salutem.

Inspeximus literas patentes Domini Jacobi, nuper Regis Angliae, patris nostri praecharissimi, de confirmatione factas in haec verba: 'JACOBUS, Dei gratia' [*etc., reciting Charter of King James I., No. XXII.*].

Confirmation of previous charters.

Nos autem cartas et literas praedictas ac omnia et singula in eisdem contenta et specificata rata habentes et grata, ea, pro nobis, heredibus et successoribus nostris, quantum in nobis est, acceptamus et approbamus, ac dilectis nobis nunc Majori,

XXIII.—*Exemplification of Charter of Henry VI. by King James I.*

1622-3, February 12.

JAMES, by the grace of God, of England, Scotland, France, and Ireland King, Defender of the Faith, to all to whom these present letters shall come, greeting. [margin: JAMES I.]

We have inspected certain letters patent of the Lord Henry the Sixth, late King of England, made to the Mayor, Bailiffs, and Burgesses of the town of Nottingham, dated the twenty-eighth day of June, in the twenty-seventh year of his reign, in the *Memoranda* of the Exchequer of our Treasurer remaining and existing in our said Exchequer in these words, to wit: 'The KING, to all to whom, etc.' [*reciting Charter of King Henry VI., No. XV.*]. [margin: *Inspeximus* of Charter of Henry VI.]

We have caused all and singular the premises to be exemplified under the seal of our Exchequer by the tenor of these presents at the request and instance of the present Mayor and Burgesses of our said town of Nottingham.

In witness whereof we have caused these our letters to be made patent. Witness our well-beloved and faithful cousin and Commissary Lionel, Earl of Middlesex, our High Treasurer of England, at Westminster, the twelfth day of February, in the year of our reign of England, France, and Ireland the twentieth, and of Scotland the fifty-sixth.

XXIV.—*Charter of King Charles I.*

1626, December 8.

CHARLES, by the grace of God, of England, Scotland, France, and Ireland King, Defender of the Faith, etc., to all to whom the present letters shall come, greeting. [margin: CHARLES I.]

We have inspected the letters patent of the Lord James, late King of England, our very dear father, of confirmation made in these words: 'JAMES, by the grace of God' [*etc., reciting Charter of King James I., No. XXII.*].

We also, esteeming the charters and letters aforesaid and all and singular the things in the same contained and specified as valid and acceptable, do, for us, our heirs and successors, so far as in us lies, accept and approve them, and do ratify and [margin: Confirmation of previous charters.]

CHARLES I. Vicecomitibus, et Burgensibus praedictae villae de Notyngham et Majori et Burgensibus ejusdem villae, heredibus et successoribus suis, tenore praesentium ratificamus et confirmamus, sicut cartae et literae praedictae in se rationabiliter testantur.

In cujus rei testimonium has literas nostras fieri fecimus patentes. Teste me ipso, apud Westmonasterium, octavo die Decembris, anno regni nostri secundo. Wolseley.

4181.

XXV.—*Charter of King Charles II.*[1]
1682, September 28.

CHARLES II.   REX, etc., omnibus ad quos, etc.

The Burgesses having surrendered their charters, owing to the ambiguities therein,

Cum villa nostra de Nottingham, in Comitatu ejusdem villae, est villa valde antiqua et populosa, et, a tempore cujus contrarii memoria hominum non existit, fuit villa incorporata, et Major, Aldermanni, Vicecomites et Burgenses villae nostrae de Nottingham praedictae, et praedecessores sui, diversas libertates, franchesias, privilegia, immunitates, et praeheminentias habuerunt et tenuerunt et usi et gavisi fuerunt, tam per chartas diversorum progenitorum et praedecessorum nostrorum, nuper Regum et Reginarum Angliae, eis praeantea factas et concessas et confirmatas, quam ratione diversarum praescriptionum et consuetudinum in eadem villa, a tempore cujus contrarii memoria hominum non existit, usitatarum; cumque nos informati sumus, quod quaedam ambiguitates in quam plurimis chartis et litteris patentibus eis praeantea factis existunt, ratione quod nonnulla in eisdem contenta non plene expressa nec verbis satis idoneis concessa fuerunt pro bono regimine, gubernatione, et commodo villae praedictae, secundum veram intentionem earundem chartarum seu literarum patentium; cumque dilecti subditi nostri Major et Burgenses villae de Nottingham praedictae nobis sursum reddiderunt literas patentes et chartas praedictas, ac omnia libertates et privilegia sua quaecunque—quam quidem sursum redditionem acceptavimus, ac per praesentes acceptamus —et humiliter supplicaverunt, quod nos omnes et singulas

---

[1] This charter, which was cancelled by the charter of William and Mary, below, No. XXVII., is here printed from the enrolment on the Patent Rolls, the original

confirm them by the tenor of these presents to our well-beloved the present Mayor, Sheriffs, and Burgesses of the aforesaid town of Nottingham and to the Mayor and Burgesses of the same town, their heirs and successors, as the charters and letters aforesaid in themselves do reasonably bear witness.

In witness whereof we have caused these our letters to be made patent. Witness myself, at Westminster, the eighth day of December, in the second year of our reign. Wolseley.

margin: CHARLES I.

4181.

XXV.—*Charter of King Charles II.*[1]
1682, September 28.

The King, etc., to all to whom, etc.

margin: CHARLES II.

Whereas our town of Nottingham, in the County of the same town, is a town very ancient and populous, and was, from time whereof the memory of man to the contrary does not exist, an incorporated town, and the Mayor, Aldermen, Sheriffs and Burgesses of our town of Nottingham aforesaid, and their predecessors, had and held and used and enjoyed divers liberties, franchises, privileges, immunities, and pre-eminences, as well by the charters of divers our progenitors and predecessors, late Kings and Queens of England, made and granted and confirmed to them heretofore, as by reason of divers prescriptions and customs used in the same town from time whereof the memory of man to the contrary does not exist; and whereas we are informed that certain ambiguities exist in many of the charters and letters patent heretofore made to them, by reason that some things contained in the same were not fully expressed nor granted in words sufficiently ample for the good rule, government, and convenience of the town aforesaid, according to the true intention of the same charters or letters patent; and whereas our well-beloved subjects the Mayor and Burgesses of the town of Nottingham aforesaid have surrendered to us the letters patent and charters aforesaid, and all their liberties and privileges whatsoever—which surrender we have accepted, and do by these presents accept—and have humbly besought that we would deign

margin: The Burgesses having surrendered theircharters, owing to the ambiguities therein,

---

having been, no doubt, destroyed when it was cancelled. The charter is badly constructed, and its grammar is occasionally very much at fault.

CHARLES II.

*have peti-
tioned us to
make them
fresh grants
of the same.*

libertates, privilegia, immunitates, et concessiones omnium progenitorum et antecessorum nostrorum eisdem Majori, Aldermannis et Burgensibus villae de Nottingham, aut praedecessoribus suis, per aliquod nomen sive aliquae nomina incorporationis facta seu concessa, de novo concedere dignaremur, cum additione augmentationum, alterationum, et explicationum quarundam libertatum, concessionum, privilegiorum, et franchesiarum prout nobis melius videbitur pro bono publico et communi utilitate ejusdem villae:

We accede to their request.

Sciatis igitur, quod nos augmentationem et emendationem villae praedictae, necnon bonum statum et gubernationem ejusdem, ut praefertur, affectantes, et volentes quod de cetero imperpetuum in eadem villa et praecinctibus ejusdem continuo habeatur unus certus et indubitatus modus et forma de et pro custodia Pacis et bono regimine et gubernatione populi ibidem, et quod villa praedicta de cetero imperpetuum sit et permaneat villa pacis et quietis, ad terrorem malorum et praemium bonorum, et quod pax nostra ceteraque facta justitiae ibidem absque ulteriori dilatione observentur; de gratia nostra speciali, et ex certa scientia et mero motu nostris, volumus, ordinavimus, constituimus, et concessimus, ac per praesentes pro nobis, heredibus et successoribus nostris, volumus, ordinamus, constituimus, declaramus, et concedimus, quod dicta villa de cetero sit et erit libera villa de se; et quod Burgenses dictae villae de Nottingham per quodcunque nomen antehac incorporati fuerunt, et successores sui, de cetero imperpetuum sint et erunt,[1] vigore praesentium, unum corpus corporatum et politicum in re, facto, et nomine per nomen 'Majoris, Aldermannorum et Burgensium villae de Nottingham in Comitatu ejusdem [villae],' ac eos per nomen 'Majoris, Aldermannorum et Burgensium villae de Nottingham in Comitatu ejusdem villae' in unum corpus corporatum et politicum in re, facto, et nomine realiter et ad plenum pro nobis, heredibus et successoribus nostris, erigimus, facimus, ordinamus, constituimus, confirmamus, et declaramus per praesentes; et quod per idem nomen habeant successionem perpetuam; et quod ipsi per nomen 'Majoris, Aldermannorum et Burgensium villae de Nottingham in Comitatu ejusdem villae' sint et erunt[1] perpetuis futuris temporibus personae habiles et in lege capaces ad

Nottingham to be a free town.

Incorporation of the same.

[1] *erunt,*] 'erint,' MS. So in other cases.

to grant anew all and singular the liberties, privileges, immuni- CHARLES II.
ties, and grants of all our progenitors and ancestors made or
granted to the same Mayor, Aldermen and Burgesses of the have petitioned us to
town of Nottingham, or to their predecessors, by any name or make them
any names of incorporation, with the addition of augmentations, fresh grants of the same.
alterations, and explanations of certain liberties, grants, privileges, and franchises as shall seem best to us for the public good
and the common utility of the same town:

Know ye therefore that we, affecting the augmentation and We accede to their request.
emendation of the town aforesaid, as well as the good estate
and government of the same, as is aforesaid, and desiring that
there shall always be in the same town and the precincts of the
same henceforth for ever a certain and undoubted manner and
form of and for the keeping of the Peace and the good rule and
government of the people there, and that the town aforesaid
henceforth for ever shall be and remain a town of peace and
quiet, to the terror of the evil and the reward of the good,
and that our peace and the other deeds of justice shall be there Nottingham to be a free town.
observed without further delay; of our especial grace, and of
our certain knowledge and mere motion, we will, have ordained,
constituted, and granted, and by these presents do for us, our
heirs and successors, will, ordain, constitute, declare, and grant
that the said town may and shall be henceforth a free town of Incorporation of the same.
itself; and that the Burgesses of the said town of Nottingham
by whatsoever name they were heretofore incorporated, and
their successors, henceforth for ever may and shall be, by the
force of these presents, a body corporate and politic in thing,
deed, and name by the name of 'the Mayor, Aldermen and
Burgesses of the town of Nottingham, in the County of the
same [town],' and do for us, our heirs and successors, erect,
make, ordain, constitute, confirm, and declare them by these
presents a body corporate and politic in thing, deed, and name
really and in full by the name of 'the Mayor, Aldermen and
Burgesses of the town of Nottingham in the County of the
same town;' and that by the same name they shall have perpetual succession; and that they by the name of 'the Mayor,
Aldermen and Burgesses of the town of Nottingham in the
County of the same town' may and shall be at all future times
persons able and capable in the law to have, acquire, receive and

habenda, perquirenda, recipienda et possidenda terras, tenementa, libertates, privilegia, jurisdictiones, franchesias, et hereditamenta, cujuscunque generis, naturae, vel speciei fuerint, necnon ad danda, concedenda, dimittenda et assignanda terras, tenementa et hereditamenta, bona et catalla, ac omnia et singula facta et res facienda et exequenda per nomen praedictum; et quod per idem nomen 'Majoris, Aldermannorum et Burgensium villae de Nottingham in Comitatu ejusdem villae' placitare et implacitari, respondere et responderi, defendere et defendi valeant et possint in quibuscunque curiis, placeis, et locis et coram quibuscunque judicibus et justitiariis ac aliis personis et officiariis nostris, ac heredum et successorum nostrorum, in omnibus sectis, querelis, placitis, causis, materiis et demandis realibus, personalibus, et mixtis, et aliis quibuscunque, tam spiritualibus, quam temporalibus, cujuscunque sint generis, naturae, seu speciei, eisdem modo et forma prout alii ligei nostri hujus regni nostri Angliae personae habiles et in lege capaces placitare et implacitari, respondere et responderi, defendere et

The Mayor and Burgesses to have a common seal. defendi, ac habere, perquirere, recipere, possidere, dare, concedere, et dimittere valeant et possint; et quod iidem Major, Aldermanni et Burgenses villae de Nottingham praedictae, et successores sui, habeant imperpetuum commune sigillum pro causis et negotiis suis et successorum suorum quibuscunque agendis deserviturum; et quod bene liceat et licebit eisdem Majori, Aldermannis et Burgensibus, et successoribus suis, sigillum illud ad libitum suum de tempore in tempus frangere, mutare, et de novo facere, prout eis melius fieri et fore videbitur.

Power to elect a Mayor, Et ulterius volumus, et per praesentes pro nobis, heredibus et successoribus nostris, concedimus et ordinamus, quod de cetero imperpetuum sit et erit infra villam praedictam unus de magis probioribus et discretioribus Burgensibus villae praedictae, in forma inferius in his praesentibus mentionata eligendus, qui erit et nominabitur 'Major' villae praedictae; quodque similiter *six other Aldermen,* sint et erunt infra villam praedictam de tempore in tempus sex Burgenses villae praedictae et continuo inhabitantes et comorantes infra villam praedictam, praeter Majorem villae praedictae, in forma inferius in his praesentibus mentionata eligendi, qui erunt et nominabuntur 'Aldermanni' villae praedictae; *18 Chief Councillors,* quodque similiter de cetero imperpetuum sint et erunt infra

possess lands, tenements, liberties, privileges, jurisdictions, franchises, and hereditaments, of whatsoever sort, nature, or kind they may be, as well as to give, grant, demise and assign lands, tenements and hereditaments, goods and chattels, and to do and execute all and singular things and deeds by the name aforesaid; and that by the same name of 'the Mayor, Aldermen and Burgesses of the town of Nottingham in the County of the same town' they may plead and be impleaded, answer and be answered, defend and be defended in whatsoever courts, places, and places and before whatsoever judges and justices and other persons and officers of us, and our heirs and successors, in all suits, plaints, pleas, causes, matters and demands real, personal, and mixed, and in others whatsoever, as well spiritual as temporal, of whatsoever sort, nature, or kind they may be, in the same manner and form as other our lieges of this our realm of England persons able and capable in the law are able and may plead and be impleaded, answer and be answered, defend and be defended, and have, acquire, receive, possess, give, grant, and demise; and that the same Mayor, Aldermen and Burgesses of the town of Nottingham aforesaid, and their successors, shall have for ever a common seal to serve for fulfilling the causes and affairs whatsoever of them and of their successors; and it may and shall be lawful to the same Mayor, Aldermen and Burgesses, and their successors, to break, change, and make anew that seal from time to time at their pleasure, as shall seem to them best to be and to be done. *The Mayor and Burgesses to have a common seal.*

And moreover we will, and do by these presents for us, our heirs and successors, grant and ordain that henceforth for ever there may and shall be within the town aforesaid one of the most approved and discreet Burgesses of the town aforesaid, to be elected in the form mentioned below in these presents, who shall be and shall be called 'the Mayor' of the town aforesaid; and that likewise there may and shall be within the town aforesaid from time to time six Burgesses of the town aforesaid and continually residing and dwelling within the town aforesaid, besides the Mayor of the town aforesaid, to be elected in the form mentioned below in these presents, who shall be and shall be called 'Aldermen' of the town aforesaid; and likewise henceforth for ever there may and shall be within the town aforesaid *Power to elect a Mayor, six other Aldermen, 18 Chief Councillors,*

Charles II.

and 6 Councillors:

who are to be called the Common Council.

villam praedictam de tempore in tempus octodecim Burgenses villae praedictae et continuo inhabitantes et comorantes infra eandem villam, in forma inferius in his praesentibus mentionata eligendi, qui erunt et nominabuntur 'Capitales Conciliarii'[1] villae praedictae; quodque similiter de cetero imperpetuum sint et erunt infra villam praedictam de tempore in tempus sex alii Burgenses villae praedictae ac continuo inhabitantes et comorantes infra eandem villam, in forma inferius in his praesentibus mentionata eligendi, qui erunt et nominabuntur 'Conciliarii' villae praedictae: qui quidem Major, Aldermanni, octodecim Capitales Conciliarii et praedicti sex Conciliarii, et successores sui, erunt et vocabuntur de cetero imperpetuum 'Commune Concilium' villae praedictae.

Power to elect two Chamberlains.

Et ulterius volumus, ac per praesentes pro nobis, heredibus et successoribus nostris, praefatis Majori, Aldermannis et Burgensibus villae praedictae, et successoribus suis, concedimus, quod de cetero imperpetuum sint et erunt in villa praedicta duo viri discreti et honesti, in forma in praesentibus inferius specificata eligendi et nominandi, qui erunt et vocabuntur 'Camerarii'

Their functions defined.

villae praedictae: qui quidem Camerarii omnia et omnimoda reditus, summas monetae, fines, amerciamenta, reventiones, proficua, commoditates et emolumenta quaecunque ad Majorem, Aldermannos et Burgenses villae praedictae, et successores suos, jure villae praedictae quoquo modo spectantia sive pertinentia valeant et possint de tempore in tempus colligere et recipere, et pro eisdem in lege postulare et recuperare in nomine et ad usum dictorum Majoris, Aldermannorum et Burgensium villae praedictae, et in camera villae praedictae conservare ad usum praedictorum Majoris, Aldermannorum et Burgensium villae illius, ac illa sic recepta et conservata ad mandatum et appunctuationem Majoris, Aldermannorum et Burgensium villae illius pro tempore existentium, vel majoris partis eorundem (quorum Majorem villae praedictae pro tempore existentem unum esse volumus), disponere et assignare.

Appointment of Mayor.

Et pro meliori executione voluntatis et concessionis nostrae in hac parte, assignavimus, nominavimus, creavimus, constituimus, et fecimus, ac per praesentes pro nobis, heredibus et successoribus nostris, assignamus, nominamus, creamus, constituimus

---

[1] *Conciliarii,*] 'Cons-,' MS. So throughout.

from time to time eighteen Burgesses of the town aforesaid and continually resident and dwelling within the same town, to be elected in the form mentioned below in these presents, who shall be and shall be called 'the Chief Councillors' of the town aforesaid; and that likewise henceforth for ever there may and shall be within the town aforesaid from time to time six other Burgesses of the town aforesaid and continually inhabiting and dwelling within the same town, to be elected in the form mentioned below in these presents, who shall be and shall be called 'Councillors' of the town aforesaid; which Mayor, Aldermen, eighteen Chief Councillors and the aforesaid six Councillors, and their successors, shall be and shall be called henceforth for ever 'the Common Council' of the town aforesaid.

Charles II.

and 6 Councillors:

who are to be called the Common Council.

And moreover we will, and do by these presents for us, our heirs and successors, grant to the aforesaid Mayor, Aldermen and Burgesses of the town aforesaid, and to their successors, that henceforth for ever there may and shall be in the town aforesaid two discreet and honest men, to be elected and nominated in the form specified below in these presents, who shall be and shall be called 'the Chamberlains' of the town aforesaid: which Chamberlains may and shall be able to collect and receive all and all manner rents, sums of money, fines, amercements, revenues, profits, commodities and emoluments whatsoever in any wise belonging or pertaining to the Mayor, Aldermen and Burgesses of the town aforesaid, and to their successors, in right of the town aforesaid, and to sue in law and recover for the same in the name and for the use of the said Mayor, Aldermen and Burgesses of the town aforesaid, and to keep the same in the chamber of the town aforesaid for the use of the aforesaid Mayor, Aldermen and Burgesses of that town, and to dispose of and assign them so received and kept at the command and appointment of the Mayor, Aldermen and Burgesses of that town for the time being, or of the major part of the same (of whom we will that the Mayor of the town aforesaid for the time being shall be one).

Power to elect two Chamberlains.

Their functions defined.

And for better execution of our will and grant in this behalf, we have assigned, nominated, created, constituted, and made, and by these presents do for us, our heirs and successors, assign, name, create, constitute, and make our well-beloved Gervase

Appointment of Mayor.

CHARLES II. et facimus dilectum nobis Gervasium Wylde, armigerum, fore et esse primum et modernum Majorem villae praedictae, continuandum in eodem officio a data praesentium usque ad festum Sancti Michaëlis Archangeli proximo futurum, et abinde quousque alius de Aldermannis villae praedictae ad officium Majoris villae illius, juxta ordinationem et provisionem in his praesentibus inferius expressam et specificatam, praefectus et juratus fuerit, si idem Gervasius Wylde tam diu vixerit.

Power to elect Mayor annually. Et ulterius volumus, ac per praesentes pro nobis, heredibus et successoribus nostris, concedimus praefatis Majori, Aldermannis et Burgensibus villae praedictae, et successoribus suis, quod Major, Aldermanni, Capitales Conciliarii, et Conciliarii inferius mentionati, et tot de iis Burgensibus qui officia Vicecomitum vel Camerariorum, inferius etiam mentionata, infra eandem villae tempore hujusmodi electionis gerunt et subeunt, vel ad aliquod tempus praeantea gessissent et subiissent,[1] sive major pars eorundem (quorum Majorem villae praedictae pro tempore existentem unum esse volumus), de tempore in tempus, perpetuis futuris temporibus, potestatem et authoritatem habeant et habebunt annuatim et quolibet anno imperpetuum, in festo Sancti Michaëlis Archangeli, eligendi et nominandi, et quod nominare et eligere possint et valeant, unum probum et discretum virum de Aldermannis villae praedictae pro tempore existentibus, qui erit Major villae praedictae a festo Sancti Michaëlis Archangeli tunc proximo sequenti[2] pro uno anno integro extunc proximo sequenti praedictum festum Sancti Michaëlis Archangeli, et abinde quousque unus alius de Aldermannis villae praedictae ad officium illud electus sit et debito modo juratus fuerit; quodque ille [qui] sic, ut praefertur, nominatus et electus fuerit in officio Majoris villae praedictae, antequam ad officium illud admittatur exequendum, sacramentum corporale in dicto festo Sancti Michaëlis Archangeli, coram Majore villae praedictae, vel Deputato suo, pro tempore existenti, ad officium illud recte, bene, et fideliter in omnibus ad officium illud tangentibus exequendum, prius praestabit; et quod, post hujusmodi sacramentum sic praestitum, officium Majoris praedicti pro uno anno integro tunc proximo sequenti exequi valeat

---

[1] The Burgesses who had filled the office of Sheriffs and Chamberlains formed the body known as 'the Clothing.' See *Borough Records*, vol. iv., p. xiii. *sqq.*

Wylde, esquire, to be the first and present Mayor of the town aforesaid, to continue in the same office from the date of these presents until the feast of Saint Michael the Archangel next to come, and from then until another of the Aldermen of the town aforesaid be advanced and sworn to the office of Mayor of that town, according to the ordinance and provision below expressed and specified in these presents, if the same Gervase Wylde live so long.

And moreover we will, and by these presents do grant for us, our heirs and successors, to the aforesaid Mayor, Aldermen and Burgesses of the town aforesaid, and to their successors, that the Mayor, Aldermen, Chief Councillors, and Councillors below mentioned, and so many of those Burgesses who bear or execute the offices of Sheriffs or Chamberlains, also mentioned below, within the same town at the time of such election, or who have borne or executed them at any time previously,[1] or the major part of them (of whom we will that the Mayor of the town aforesaid for the time being shall be one), shall and may have, from time to time, at all future times, power and authority to elect and nominate annually and in every year for ever, in the feast of Saint Michael the Archangel, and that they may and shall be able to elect and name, an approved and discreet man of the Aldermen of the town aforesaid for the time being, who shall be Mayor of the town aforesaid from the feast of Saint Michael the Archangel then next following[2] for one whole year then next following the aforesaid feast of Saint Michael the Archangel, and from then until another of the Aldermen of the town aforesaid be elected and in due manner sworn to that office; and that he who shall thus be named and elected to the office of Mayor of the town aforesaid, as is aforesaid, shall, before he be admitted to execute that office, first take his bodily oath in the said feast of Saint Michael the Archangel, before the Mayor of the town aforesaid, or his Deputy, for the time being, to execute everything pertaining to that office rightly, well, and faithfully; and that, after he has taken such oath, he may and shall be able to execute the

Power to elect Mayor annually.

---

[2] This must be a mistake for 'the same feast of Saint Michael the Archangel.' According to the above wording the Mayor would be elected a year before his term of office commenced; whereas he entered upon his office forthwith.

CHARLES II.

The Mayor may appoint a Deputy.

et possit, et abinde quousque unus alius de Aldermannis praedictis in officium Majoris electus et praefectus fuerit. Et ulterius volumus, ac per praesentes pro nobis, heredibus et successoribus nostris, concedimus praefatis Majori, Aldermannis et Burgensibus villae praedictae, et successoribus suis, quod si contigerit Majorem villae praedictae pro tempore existentem sic aegritudine laborare quod necessaria negotia villae praedictae attendere non possit, aut villam praedictam pro aliqua causa rationabili egredi,[1] quod[2] tunc et toties de tempore in tempus liceat et licebit Majori villae praedictae pro tempore existenti, sic aegritudine laboranti aut pro aliqua causa rationabili absenti, eligere, deputare, et constituere quendam alium e sex Aldermannis praedictis fore et esse Deputatum Majorem villae praedictae, continuandum in eodem officio Deputati Majoris villae praedictae in absentia aut aegritudine Majoris villae praedictae pro tempore existentis; qui quidem Deputatus Major villae praedictae sic, ut praefertur, deputandus et constituendus in Deputatum Majorem villae praedictae pro tempore existentem omnia et singula, quae ad officium Majoris villae illius infra villam praedictam pertinent et pertinere debent facienda et exequenda, facere et exequi valeat et possit durante bene placito Majoris villae praedictae, in absentia vel aegritudine ejusdem Majoris pro tempore existentis, adeo plene, libere, et integre prout Major villae praedictae pro tempore existens, si praesens esset, facere et exequi valeat et possit; et sic toties quoties casus sic acciderit.

In case the Mayor die in his year of office, they may elect a successor to hold office for the unexpired term.

Et volumus, ac per praesentes pro nobis, heredibus et successoribus nostris, concedimus Majori, Aldermannis et Burgensibus villae praedictae, et successoribus suis, quod si contigerit Majorem villae praedictae pro tempore existentem, aliquo tempore infra unum annum postquam ad officium Majoris villae praedictae sic, ut praefertur, nominatus, electus, praefectus, et juratus fuerit, obire, aut ab officio illo amoveri, quod tunc et toties bene liceat et licebit Aldermannis, Capitalibus Conciliariis, Conciliariis, et tot de iis Burgensibus qui officia Vicecomitum vel Camerariorum infra eandem villam tempore hujusmodi electionis gerunt vel subeunt, vel ad aliquod tempus praeantea gessissent et subiissent, vel majori parti eorundem, convenire et assemblare in communi loco

---

[1] This seems to be intended for *ingredi*, 'enter.'
[2] A redundant *quod* occurs in the MS. here and in the similar passages below.

office of the aforesaid Mayor for one whole year then next following, and from then until another one of the Aldermen aforesaid be elected and advanced to the office of Mayor. And moreover we will, and do by these presents for us, our heirs and successors, grant to the aforesaid Mayor, Aldermen and Burgesses of the town aforesaid, and to their successors, that if it happen that the Mayor of the town aforesaid for the time being shall so labour with illness as to be unable to attend to the necessary affairs of the aforesaid town, or to go out of¹ the town aforesaid for any reasonable cause, then and as many times from time to time it may and shall be lawful for the Mayor of the town aforesaid for the time being, so labouring with illness or being absent for any reasonable cause, to elect, depute, and appoint one other of the six Aldermen aforesaid to be the Deputy-Mayor of the town aforesaid, to continue in the same office of Deputy-Mayor of the town aforesaid in the absence or illness of the Mayor of the town aforesaid for the time being; which Deputy-Mayor of the town aforesaid to be thus deputed and appointed Deputy-Mayor of the town aforesaid for the time being, as is aforesaid, may and shall be able to do and execute within the town aforesaid all and singular the things that pertain and ought to pertain to be done and executed to the office of Mayor of that town, during the pleasure of the Mayor of the town aforesaid, in the absence or illness of the same Mayor for the time being, as fully, freely, and wholly as the Mayor of the town aforesaid for the time being might and should be able to do and execute them if he were present; and so as often as the case shall so happen. And we will, and do by these presents for us, our heirs and successors, grant to the Mayor, Aldermen and Burgesses of the town aforesaid, and to their successors, that if it happen that the Mayor of the town aforesaid for the time being die or be removed from that office at any time within one year after he have been thus nominated, elected, advanced, and sworn to the office of Mayor of the town aforesaid, as is beforesaid, then and at all times it may and shall be lawful to the Aldermen, Chief Councillors, Councillors, and so many of those Burgesses who bear or execute the offices of Sheriffs or Chamberlains within the same town at the time of such election, or who have borne or executed them at any time previously, or

The Mayor may appoint a Deputy.

In case the Mayor die in his year of office, they may elect a successor to hold office for the unexpired term.

CHARLES II.

vocato '*Guihald*,' aut alio loco convenienti, infra villam praedictam infra duodecim dies proximo post notitiam mortis aut amotionis dicti Majoris, et ibidem unum alium de Aldermannis villae praedictae in officium Majoris villae praedictae nominare, eligere, et praeficere, secundum ordinationem et provisionem superius in praesentibus declaratas; et quod ille sic eligendus et praeficiendus in officium Majoris villae praedictae, officium illud habeat et exerceat durante residuo ejusdem anni, sacramento corporali in forma praedicta prius praestando; et sic toties quoties casus sic acciderit.

Appointment of Aldermen.

Assignavimus etiam, nominavimus, creavimus, constituimus, et fecimus, ac per praesentes pro nobis, heredibus et successoribus nostris, assignamus, nominamus, creamus, constituimus, et facimus dilectos nobis Radulfum Edge, Christopherum Hall, Johannem Parker, Gervasium Rippon, Willelmum Toplady, et Willelmum Petty, generosos, fore et esse modernos Aldermannos villae praedictae, continuandos in eisdem officiis durantibus vitis suis naturalibus, nisi interim pro mala gubernatione sive male se gerendo in ea parte, aut pro aliqua causa rationabili, ab officiis illis amoti erunt, aut eorum aliquis vel aliqui amoti erunt vel amotus erit.

Provision for election of their successors.

Et ulterius volumus, quod quandocunque contigerit aliquem vel aliquos de praedictis Aldermannis villae praedictae, sive successoribus suis, de tempore in tempus obire, aut ab officiis suis Aldermannorum villae praedictae amoveri,— quos quidem Aldermannos villae praedictae, seu eorum aliquem, vel aliquos, se non bene gerentes in officiis illis amobiles esse volumus ad bene placitum Majoris et residuorum Aldermannorum, Capitalium Conciliariorum, et sex Conciliariorum villae praedictae, vel majoris partis eorundem (quorum Majorem villae praedictae pro tempore existentem unum esse volumus),— quod tunc et toties bene liceat et licebit praedictis Majori, residuis Aldermannorum, Capitalibus Conciliariis, Conciliariis, et tot de iis Burgensibus qui officium Vicecomitum vel Camerariorum infra eandem villam tempore hujusmodi electionis gerunt et subeunt, vel ad aliquod tempus praeantea gessissent et subiissent, vel majori parti eorundem (quorum Majorem pro tempore existentem unum esse volumus), unum alium, vel plures alios, de Capitalibus Conciliariis villae praedictae in his praesentibus

to the major part of them, to convene and assemble in the common place called 'Guild Hall,' or in any other convenient place, within the town aforesaid within twelve days next after notice of the death or amoval of the said Mayor, and to there name, elect, and advance one other of the Aldermen of the town aforesaid to the office of Mayor of the town aforesaid, according to the ordinance and provision above declared in these presents; and he to be thus elected and advanced to the office of Mayor of the town aforesaid shall have and exercise that office during the remainder of the same year, having previously taken his bodily oath in form aforesaid: and so as often as the case shall so happen.

We have assigned, named, created, constituted, and made, and do by these presents for us, our heirs and successors, assign, name, create, constitute, and make our well-beloved Ralph Edge, Christopher Hall, John Parker, Gervase Rippon, William Toplady, and William Petty, gentlemen, to be the present Aldermen of the town aforesaid, to continue in the same offices during their natural lives, unless in the meantime they be amoved, or any one or more of them be amoved from those offices for their bad government or misconduct in that behalf, or for any other reasonable cause. And moreover we will, that whenever it shall happen from time to time that any one or more of the aforesaid Aldermen of the town aforesaid, or of their successors, shall die, or be amoved from their offices of Aldermen of the town aforesaid—which Aldermen of the town aforesaid, or any one or more of them, not conducting themselves well in their offices we will shall be amovable at the will of the Mayor and the rest of the Aldermen, Chief Councillors, and six Councillors of the town aforesaid, or of the greater part of them (of whom we will that the Mayor of the town aforesaid for the time being shall be one)—then and so often it may and shall be lawful to the aforesaid Mayor, the rest of the Aldermen, the Chief Councillors, Councillors, and so many of the Burgesses who bear or execute the offices of Sheriffs or Chamberlains within the same town at the time of such election, or who have at any time previously borne or executed such office, or to the major part of them (of whom we will that the Mayor for the time being shall be one), to elect,

CHARLES II. postea nominatis in loco, sive locis, ipsius, vel ipsorum, Aldermanni, vel Aldermannorum, villae praedictae sic mori vel amoveri contingentium, eligere, nominare, et praeficere, ad supplendum praedictum numerum sex Aldermannorum villae praedictae; quodque ille, sive illi, sic, ut praefertur, ad officium Aldermanni, vel Aldermannorum, villae praedictae electus et praefectus, electi et praefecti, erit et erunt de numero praedictorum sex Aldermannorum villae praedictae; et hoc de tempore in tempus toties quoties casus sic acciderit.

Appointment of Chief Councillors. Assignavimus etiam, nominavimus, creavimus, constituimus, et fecimus, ac per praesentes pro nobis, heredibus et successoribus nostris, assignamus, nominamus, creamus, constituimus, et facimus dilectos nobis Edmundum Mabot, Willelmum Mabot, Robertum Coulson, Hugonem Walker, Willelmum Hardy, Vincentium Beverley, Carolum Chadwick, Willelmum Unwin, Francum Sulley, Robertum Peach, Samuelem Hooke, Stephanum Broome, Edwardum Wilkinson, Jacobum Villiers, Robertum Worthley, Willelmum Woolhouse, Johannem Malyn, et Johannem Whitby fore et esse modernos Capitales Conciliarios villae praedictae, continuandos in eisdem officiis durantibus vitis suis naturalibus respective, nisi interim pro mala gubernatione sive male se gerendo in officiis suis praedictis, aut pro aliqua alia causa rationabili, amoti fuerint, aut eorum aliqui, vel aliquis,

Provision for election of their successors. amotus erit, vel amoti erunt. Et ulterius volumus, ac per praesentes pro nobis, heredibus et successoribus nostris, concedimus praefatis Majori, Aldermannis et Burgensibus villae praedictae, et successoribus suis imperpetuum, quod, quandocunque contigerit aliquem vel aliquos de Capitalibus Conciliariis villae praedictae, seu aliquos successorum suorum, obire, aut ab officiis suis Capitalium Conciliariorum villae praedictae amoveri,—quos quidem Capitales Conciliarios villae praedictae pro tempore existentes, vel successores suos, sive eorum aliquem, vel aliquos, se non bene gerentem, aut gerentes, in officiis illis amobiles esse volumus ad bene placitum Majoris, Aldermannorum et Communium[1] Conciliariorum villae praedictae pro tempore existentium, vel majoris partis eorundem (quorum Majorem villae praedictae pro tempore existentem unum esse volumus),—quod tunc et toties bene liceat et licebit praefatis Majori, Aldermannis et Burgensibus villae praedictae pro tempore existentibus, et

name, and advance one other, or others, of the Chief Councillors of the town aforesaid named hereafter in these presents in the place, or places, of such Alderman, or Aldermen, of the town aforesaid so happening to die or be amoved, to make up the aforesaid number of six Aldermen of the town aforesaid; and that he, or they, thus elected and advanced to the office of Alderman, or Aldermen, of the town aforesaid, shall be of the number of the aforesaid six Aldermen of the town aforesaid; and this from time to time as often as the case shall so happen.

Charles II.

We have assigned, named, created, constituted, and made, and do by these presents for us, our heirs and successors, assign, name, create, constitute, and make our well-beloved Edmund Mabot, William Mabot, Robert Coulson, Hugh Walker, William Hardy, Vincent Beverley, Charles Chadwick, William Unwin, Frank Sulley, Robert Peach, Samuel Hook, Stephen Broom, Edward Wilkinson, James Villiers, Robert Worthley, William Woolhouse, John Malin, and John Whitby to be the present Chief Councillors of the town aforesaid, to respectively continue in the same offices during their natural lives, unless in the meantime they, or any one or more of them, be amoved for their bad government or misconduct in their aforesaid offices, or for any other reasonable cause. And moreover we will, and do grant by these presents for us, our heirs and successors, to the aforesaid Mayor, Aldermen and Burgesses of the town aforesaid, and to their successors for ever, that whensoever it shall happen that any one or more of the Chief Councillors of the town aforesaid, or any of their successors, die or be amoved from their offices of Chief Councillors of the town aforesaid—which Chief Councillors of the town aforesaid for the time being, or their successors, or any one or more of them not well behaving himself, or themselves, in those offices we will shall be amovable at the pleasure of the Mayor, Aldermen and Common Councillors of the town aforesaid for the time being, or of the major part of them (of whom we will that the Mayor of the town aforesaid for the time being shall be one)—then and as often it may and shall be lawful to the aforesaid Mayor, Aldermen and Burgesses of the town aforesaid for the time being, and to their successors, or to

Appointment of Chief Councillors.

Provision for election of their successors.

---

¹ *Communium,*] ' Communis,' MS.

CHARLES II. successoribus suis, vel majori parti eorundem (quorum Majorem pro tempore existentem unum esse volumus), unum alium, vel plures, de Burgensibus villae praedictae in loco, sive locis, ipsius, vel ipsorum Capitalium Conciliariorum villae praedictae sic mori vel amoveri contingentium, eligere, nominare, et praeficere, ad supplendum praedictum numerum octodecim Capitalium Conciliariorum villae praedictae; quodque ille, sive illi, sic ut praefertur ad officium Capitalis Conciliarii villae praedictae electus et praefectus, aut electi et praefecti, erit et erunt de numero octodecim Capitalium Conciliariorum villae praedictae; et hoc toties quoties casus sic acciderit.

Appointment of the six Councillors. Assignavimus etiam, nominavimus, creavimus, constituimus, et fecimus, ac per praesentes pro nobis, heredibus et successoribus nostris, assignamus, nominamus, creamus, constituimus et facimus dilectos nobis Willelmum Jackson, Thomam Lee, Johannem Unwin, Ricardum Wright, Henricum Hardy, et Johannem Shipman fore et esse modernos Conciliarios villae praedictae, continuandos in eisdem officiis durantibus vitis suis naturalibus respective, nisi interim pro mala gubernatione sive male se gerendo in officiis suis praedictis, aut pro aliqua alia causa rationabili amoti fuerint, aut eorum aliqui, vel aliquis, amoti *Provision for* erunt, vel amotus erit. Et ulterius volumus, ac per praesentes *the election of their successors.* pro nobis, heredibus et successoribus nostris, concedimus praefatis Majori, Aldermannis et Burgensibus villae praedictae, et successoribus suis imperpetuum, quod quandocunque contigerit aliquem vel aliquos de dictis sex Conciliariis villae praedictae, seu aliquos successorum suorum, obire, aut ab officiis suis Conciliariorum villae praedictae amoveri,—quos quidem Conciliarios villae praedictae[1] pro tempore existentes, et successores suos, sive eorum aliquem vel aliquos se non bene gerentem, aut gerentes, in officiis illis amobiles esse volumus—quod tunc et toties bene liceat et licebit praefatis Majori, Aldermannis et Burgensibus villae praedictae pro tempore existentibus, et successoribus suis, vel majori parti eorundem (quorum Majorem pro tempore existentem unum esse volumus), unum alium, vel plures, de Burgensibus villae praedictae in loco, sive locis, ipsius vel ipsorum Conciliariorum villae praedictae sic mori vel amoveri contingentium, eligere, nominare, et praeficere ad supplendum numerum sex Conciliariorum villae praedictae;

the major part of them (of whom we will that the Mayor for the time being shall be one), to elect, name, and advance one other, or more, of the Burgesses of the town aforesaid in the place, or places, of such Chief Councillor, or Councillors, of the town aforesaid so happening to die or be amoved, to make up the aforesaid number of eighteen Chief Councillors of the town aforesaid; and that he, or they, so elected and advanced to the office of Chief Councillor of the town aforesaid, shall be of the number of the eighteen Chief Councillors of the town aforesaid; and this so often as the case shall so happen.

We have also assigned, named, created, constituted, and made, and do by these presents for us, our heirs and successors, assign, name, create, constitute and make our well-beloved William Jackson, Thomas Lee, John Unwin, Richard Wright, Henry Hardy, and John Shipman to be the present Councillors of the town aforesaid, to continue respectively in the same offices during their natural lives, unless they, or any one of them, be amoved in the meantime for bad government or evil conduct in their aforesaid offices, or for any other reasonable cause. And moreover we will, and do grant by these presents for us, our heirs and successors, to the aforesaid Mayor, Aldermen and Burgesses of the town aforesaid, and to their successors for ever, that whenever it shall happen that any one or more of the said six Councillors of the town aforesaid, or any of their successors, shall die or be amoved from their offices of Councillors of the town aforesaid—which Councillors of the town aforesaid for the time being, and their successors, or any one or more of them not behaving themselves well in those offices we will shall be amovable—then and at all times it may and shall be lawful to the aforesaid Mayor, Aldermen and Burgesses of the town aforesaid for the time being, and their successors, or the major part of them (of whom we will the Mayor for the time being shall be one) to elect, name, and advance one other, or more, of the Burgesses of the town aforesaid in the place, or places, of that, or those, Councillors of the town aforesaid so happening to die or be amoved, to fill up the number of six Councillors of the

---

[1] The Roll here needlessly interlines *amoveri quos quidem Conciliarios villae praedictae.*

CHARLES II. quodque ille, sive illi, sic, ut praefertur, ad officium Conciliariorum villae praedictae electus et praefectus, aut electi et praefecti, erit et erunt de numero sex Conciliariorum villae praedictae; et hoc toties quoties casus sic acciderit.

Appointment of Chamberlains.

Assignavimus etiam, nominavimus, creavimus, constituimus, et fecimus, ac per praesentes pro nobis, heredibus et successoribus nostris, assignamus, nominamus, creamus, constituimus, et facimus dilectos nobis Johannem Peake et Johannem Uthwayte fore et esse modernos Camerarios villae praedictae, continuandos in officiis Camerariorum usque ad festum Sancti Michaëlis Archangeli proximo sequens datum praesentium, et abinde quousque duo alii de sex Conciliariis, vel aliis Burgensibus villae praedictae non existentibus de numero octodecim Capitalium Conciliariorum villae praedictae, in officia Camerariorum electi et praefecti fuerint; et ad verum compotum inde reddendum praefatis Majori, Aldermannis et Communibus Conciliariis villae

Provision for the election of their successors.

praedictae; et hoc toties quoties eis expedire videbitur. Et quod de tempore in tempus et ad omnia tempora post praedictum festum Sancti Michaëlis Archangeli, mortem vel amotionem praedictorum Johannis Peake et Johannis Uthwayte, vel alterius eorum, vel alicujus seu aliquorum successorum suorum, Major, Aldermanni et Commune[s] Conciliarii villae praedictae pro tempore existentes, vel major pars eorum (quorum Majorem ejusdem villae pro tempore existentem unum esse volumus), unum alium virum, vel duos viros discretos et honestos, de praedictis sex Conciliariis vel Burgensibus villae praedictae non existentibus Capitalibus Conciliariis ejusdem villae, in Camerarios villae praedictae eligere, nominare, et praeficere valeant et possint; quodque ille, sive illi, qui in Camerarios villae praedictae sic, ut praefertur, electus, praefectus, et nominatus fuerit, vel electi, praefecti, et nominati fuerint, officia illa Camerariorum villae praedictae exercere et gaudere valeant et possint, valeat et possit, pro uno anno integro extunc proximo sequenti, et abinde quousque unum alium, vel duo alii, ex sex Conciliariis vel aliis Burgensibus villae praedictis non existentibus de numero octodecim Capitalium Conciliariorum villae praedictae, ad officia praedicta Camerariorum villae praedictae debito modo electi et praefecti fuerit vel fuerint; et hoc toties quoties casus sic acciderit: nisi interim pro mala gubernatione sive male se

town aforesaid; and that he, or they, so elected and advanced to the office of Councillors of the town aforesaid shall be of the number of the six Councillors of the town aforesaid; and this so often as the case shall so happen.

We have also assigned, named, created, constituted, and made, and do by these presents for us, our heirs and successors, assign, name, create, appoint, and make our well-beloved John Peake and John Uthwaite to be the present Chamberlains of the town aforesaid, to continue in the offices of Chamberlains until the feast of Saint Michael the Archangel next following the date of these presents, and from then until two others of the six Councillors, or other Burgesses of the town aforesaid not being of the number of the eighteen Chief Councillors of the town aforesaid, be elected and advanced to the offices of Chamberlains; and to render true account thereof to the aforesaid Mayor, Aldermen and Common Council of the town aforesaid; and this as many times as shall seem fit to them. And that from time to time and at all times after the aforesaid feast of Saint Michael the Archangel, the death or amoval of the aforesaid John Peake and John Uthwaite, or either of them, or any one or more of their successors, the Mayor, Aldermen and Common Council of the town aforesaid for the time being, or the major part of them (of whom we will that the Mayor of the same town for the time being shall be one), may and shall be able to elect, name, and advance one other man, or two discreet and honest men, of the aforesaid six Councillors or of the Burgesses of the town aforesaid not being Chief Councillors of the same town, as Chamberlains of the town aforesaid; and that he, or they, who shall be thus elected, advanced, and named as Chamberlains of the town aforesaid, as is beforesaid, may and shall be able to exercise and enjoy those offices of Chamberlains of the town aforesaid for one whole year then next following, and from then until one other, or two others, of the six Councillors or other Burgesses of the town aforesaid not being of the number of the eighteen Chief Councillors of the town aforesaid, be in due manner elected and advanced to the aforesaid offices of Chamberlains of the town aforesaid; and this so many times as the case shall so happen: unless they, or either of them, be amoved from their offices by the

CHARLES II. gerendo in ea parte, aut pro aliqua causa rationabili, ab officiis illis amoti erunt, aut eorum alter, amoti erunt, vel amotus erit, per Majorem, Aldermannos et Communes Conciliarios villae praedictae, vel majorem partem eorundem (quorum Majorem pro tempore existentem unum esse volumus).

Appointment of Coroners.

Et volumus, ac per praesentes pro nobis, heredibus et successoribus nostris, concedimus praefatis Majori, Aldermannis et Burgensibus villae praedictae, et successoribus suis, quod de cetero imperpetuum ipsi, et successores sui, habeant et habebunt infra villam praedictam duos honestos et discretos viros qui erunt et vocabuntur 'Coronatores' villae praedictae, sicut antiquo habuerunt, et modo habent, qui erunt perpetuis futuris temporibus assistentes, consulentes, et auxiliantes Majori villae praedictae; et quod praedicti Coronatores villae praedictae pro tempore existentes facient omnia et singula infra villam praedictam, limites et praecinctus ejusdem, quae aliquis Coronator vel aliqui Coronatores virtute officii illius facere et exequi potuit aut debuit, possint aut debent, et non aliter. Et pro meliori executione voluntatis et concessionis nostrae in hac parte, assignamus, nominamus, constituimus, et facimus dilectos nobis Robertum Worthley et Willelmum Woolhouse, generosos, fore et esse primos et modernos Coronatores villae praedictae durantibus vitis suis naturalibus, nisi interim illi, sive eorum alter, pro se male gerendo in officio illo amoti fuerint vel fuerit per Majorem et Commune[s] Concil[iarios] villae praedictae pro tempore existentes. Et volumus, quod praedicti Robertus Worthley et Willelmus Woolhouse, et quique Coronatores villae praedictae imposterum eligendi, antequam ad officia Coronatorum praedictorum admittantur aut admittatur, sacramentum corporale super sacrosancta Dei Evangelia[1] coram Majore villae praedictae pro tempore existenti, ad omnia et singula, quae ad officium Coronatorum villae praedictae pertinent, recte, bene, et fideliter in omnibus et per omnia facienda et exequenda, praestabunt, et praestabit: cui quidem Majori villae praedictae pro tempore existenti hujusmodi sacramentum administrandi pro nobis, heredibus et successoribus nostris, authoritatem et potestatem concedimus per praesentes. Et ulterius volumus, ac per praesentes pro nobis, heredibus et successoribus nostris, concedimus Majori, Aldermannis et Burgensibus villae praedictae

Provision for the election of their successors.

Mayor, Aldermen and Common Councillors of the town afore- CHARLES II.
said, or the major part of them (of whom we will that the
Mayor for the time being shall be one), for their bad government or misconduct in this behalf, or for any other reasonable
cause.

And moreover we will, and do grant by these presents for Appointment of Coroners.
us, our heirs and successors, to the aforesaid Mayor, Aldermen
and Burgesses of the town aforesaid, and to their successors,
that they and their successors, may and shall have henceforth
for ever within the town aforesaid two honest and discreet men
who shall be and shall be called 'Coroners' of the town aforesaid, as they had of old, and now have, who shall be assisting,
counselling, and helping to the Mayor of the town aforesaid in
future times; and that the aforesaid Coroners of the town aforesaid for the time being shall do all and singular the things
within the town aforesaid, the limits and precincts of the same,
that any Coroner or Coroners might or should do and execute
by virtue of that office, and not otherwise. And for the better
execution of our will and grant in this behalf, we assign, name,
constitute, and make our well-beloved Robert Worthley and
William Woolhouse, gentlemen, to be the first and present
Coroners of the town aforesaid during their natural lives, unless
they, or either of them, be amoved in the meantime by the Mayor
and Common Councillors of the town aforesaid for the time being
for evil conduct in that office. And we will, that the aforesaid
Robert Worthley and William Woolhouse and every Coroner of
the town aforesaid to be hereafter elected shall, before he or
they be admitted to the offices of Coroners aforesaid, take
bodily oath on the holy Gospels¹ of God, before the Mayor of
the town aforesaid for the time being, to rightly, well, and faithfully do and execute in all things and through all things all and
everything that pertains to the office of Coroner of the town
aforesaid: to which Mayor of the town aforesaid for the time
being we grant for us, our heirs and successors, by these presents
authority and power to administer such oath. And moreover Provision for the election
we will, and do grant by these presents for us, our heirs and of their successors, to the Mayor, Aldermen and Burgesses of the town cessors.
aforesaid for the time being, and to their successors, that it may

¹ *Evangelia*,] 'evangelii,' MS.

pro tempore existentibus, et successoribus suis, quod de tempore in tempus, post mortem vel amotionem praedictorum Roberti Worthley et Willelmi Woolhouse, vel alterius eorum, bene liceat et licebit Majori, Aldermannis et Capitalibus Conciliariis, sex Conciliariis, et tot de iis Burgensibus qui officia Vicecomitum et Camerariorum tempore hujusmodi electionis gerunt et subeunt, aut praeantea gesserunt aut subierunt, vel majori parti eorum (quorum Majorem pro tempore existentem unum esse volumus), unum virum, vel duos viros, in officium Coronatorum villae praedictae eligere et praeficere, continuandos in officiis dictorum Coronatorum durantibus vitis suis naturalibus, nisi pro se male gerendo in officiis illis amoti fuerint, ut praedictum est; et sic toties quoties casus sic acciderit.

Power to fine those who refuse to accept office.
Et si aliquis imposterum sic electus in officium Majoris villae praedictae, aut in officio sive loco Aldermanni, Vicecomitis, Capitalis Conciliarii, [Conciliarii,] vel Camerarii, aut in aliquod aliud officium sive locum infra villam praedictam, cui electio illa notificata erit, recusaverit accipere super se officium sive officia praedicta, aut jura[mentum] et alia requisita in ea parte praestare et performare, sine causa rationabili, quod tunc et in quolibet tali casu bene liceat et licebit eisdem Majori, Communi Concillio villae praedictae, vel majori parti eorundem pro tempore existentibus (quorum Majorem pro tempore existentem unum esse volumus), de tempore in tempus taxare et imponere tales rationabiles fines super quamlibet hujusmodi personam sic recusantem, quales eisdem Majori et Communi Concilio villae praedictae, aut majori parti eorundem, rationabiliter videbitur

Grant of fines so imposed.
expediendi; et ad hujusmodi fines et fines sic de tempore in tempus taxatos et impositos per districtionem et venditionem bonorum et catallorum cujuslibet hujusmodi personae et personarum sic recusantium, aut per actionem debiti, seu alio legali modo quocunque, de tempore in tempus ad et pro usu et proficuo dictorum Majoris, Aldermannorum et Burgensium ejusdem villae, levare, percipere, et detinere valeant et possint, sine molestatione sive impedimento nostri, heredum vel successorum nostrorum; et hoc absque aliquo compoto seu alia re quacunque nobis, heredibus vel successoribus nostris, proinde reddendo vel solvendo.

Power to have a Recorder.
Et volumus, ac per praesentes pro nobis, heredibus et

and shall be lawful to the Mayor, Aldermen and Chief Coun- cillors, six Councillors, and so many of the Burgesses who bear or execute the offices of Sheriffs and Chamberlains at the time of such election, or who have borne or executed them at any time previously, or the major part of them (of whom we will that the Mayor for the time being shall be one) to elect and advance, from time to time, after the death or amoval of the aforesaid Robert Worthley and William Woolhouse, or of either of them, one man, or two men, to the office of Coroners of the town aforesaid, to continue in the offices of the said Coroners during their natural lives, unless they be amoved for their evil conduct in those offices, as is beforesaid; and this so often as the case shall so happen.

And hereafter if any one so elected to the office of Mayor of the town aforesaid, or to the office or place of an Alderman, Sheriff, Chief Councillor, [Councillor,] or Chamberlain, or to any other office or place within the town aforesaid, to whom that election has been notified, shall refuse, without reasonable cause, to take upon himself the office or offices aforesaid, or to take and perform the oath and other requisites in that behalf, that then and in every such case it may and shall be lawful to the same Mayor, Common Council of the town aforesaid, or the major part of them for the time being (of whom we will that the Mayor for the time being shall be one), to tax and impose from time to time such reasonable fines upon each such person so refusing as shall reasonably appear to be expedient to the same Mayor and Common Council of the town aforesaid, or to the major part of them; and that they may be able to levy, receive, and retain such fines and fines so from time to time taxed and imposed by distraint and sale of the goods and chattels of every such person and persons so refusing, or by action of debt, or in any other legal manner whatsoever, from time to time to and for the use and profit of the said Mayor, Aldermen and Burgesses of the same town, without molestation or impediment from us, our heirs and successors; and this without rendering or paying therefor to us, our heirs or successors, any account or anything else whatsoever.

Power to fine those who refuse to accept office.

Grant of fines so imposed.

And we will, and do grant by these presents for us, our heirs

Power to have a Recorder.

> CHARLES II. successoribus nostris, concedimus praefatis Majori, Aldermannis et Burgensibus villae praedictae pro tempore existentibus, et successoribus suis, quod ipsi, et successores sui, de cetero imperpetuum habeant et habebunt in et pro villa praedicta unum virum praeclarum et discretum, in forma inferius in his praesentibus expressa [eligendum], qui erit et nominabitur 'Recordator' villae praedictae, ad omnia et singula agenda et exequenda quae ad officium Recordatoris in eadem villa, seu in aliqua alia villa sive loco incorporato,[1] pertinent.

Power to have a Common Clerk.

> Ac etiam, quod praedicti Major, Aldermanni et Burgenses villae praedictae, et successores sui, de cetero imperpetuum habeant et habebunt in villa praedicta unum alium virum in legibus Angliae eruditum, in forma inferius in his praesentibus [expressa] nominandum et eligendum, qui erit et vocabitur

His duties defined.

> 'Communis Clericus' villae praedictae, ad facienda et exequenda omnia et singula recognitiones captas, recognitas, et recognoscendas coram Majore et aliis Justitiariis Pacis villae praedictae, in praesentia praedictorum Majoris et Justitiariorum, et easdem sic captas et recognitas transcribere et in pergamenam redigere, et ad scribendas et intrandas omnes indenturas apprent[iciae], et querelas, placita, actiones, ac alia originalia et judicialia brevia et processus quaecunque, et judicia et considerationes superinde, in Curia de Recordo infra villam praedictam, libertates, bundas, et praecinctus ejusdem, et ad ea omnia exequenda ad onus et officium suum designanda, et quae aliquis Communis Clericus infra eandem villam, seu aliquam aliam villam vel burgum incorporatum infra regnum nostrum Angliae, virtute officii illius, exequi possit et valeat; quodque dictus Communis Clericus omnia et singula feoda, regarda, et proficua pro scriptione et intratione praedictis, ac omnia alia feoda et proficua, quae ad locum Communis Clerici praedicti [pertinent], habeat et percipiat.[2]

Appointment of Recorder.

> Assignavimus etiam, nominavimus, constituimus, et fecimus, ac per praesentes, pro nobis, heredibus et successoribus nostris, assignamus, nominamus, constituimus, et facimus perquam fidelem et perquam sincere dilectum consanguineum et Conciliarium nostrum Henricum, Ducem de Novo Castro, in legibus hujus regni nostri Angliae peritum, fore et esse modernum Recordatorem villae praedictae, ad omnia et singula agenda et

and successors, to the aforesaid Mayor, Aldermen and Burgesses of the town aforesaid for the time being, and to their successors, that they, and their successors, may and shall have henceforth for ever in and for the town aforesaid one distinguished and discreet man, to be elected in the form below expressed in these presents, who shall be and shall be called 'the Recorder' of the town aforesaid, to do and execute all and singular the things that pertain to the office of Recorder in the same town, or in any other town or place incorporated.

And also that the aforesaid Mayor, Aldermen and Burgesses of the town aforesaid, and their successors, may and shall have henceforth for ever in the town aforesaid one other man learned in the laws of England, to be nominated and elected in the form below [expressed] in these presents, who shall be and shall be called 'the Common Clerk' of the town aforesaid, to do and execute all and singular the recognizances taken, recognized, and to be recognized before the Mayor and the other Justices of the Peace of the town aforesaid, in the presence of the aforesaid Mayor and Justices, and to transcribe and enter them on parchment when so taken and recognized, and to write and enter all indentures of apprenticeship, and plaints, pleas, actions, and other original and judicial writs and processes whatsoever, and judgments and decisions thereupon, in the Court of Record within the town aforesaid, the liberties, bounds, and precincts of the same, and to execute all those things to be designated for his charge and office, and that any Common Clerk may and is able to execute, by virtue of his office, within the same town, or within any other town or incorporated borough, within our realm of England; and that the said Common Clerk shall have and receive all and singular the fees, rewards, and profits for the writing and entering aforesaid, and all other fees and profits that [pertain] to the place of the Common Clerk aforesaid.

We have also assigned, named, appointed and made, and do by these presents, for us, our heirs and successors, assign, name, appoint, and make our very faithful and very dearly beloved cousin and our Councillor Henry, Duke of Newcastle, learned in the laws of this our kingdom of England, to be the

Charles II.

Power to have a Common Clerk.

His duties defined.

Appointment of Recorder.

---

¹ *incorporato*,] 'incorporeat.,' MS. ² *percipiat*,] 'praecipiat,' MS.

exequenda, quae ad officium Recordatoris in eadem villa, vel in aliqua alia villa sive loco incorporato infra regnum nostrum Angliae pertinent, continuandum in eodem officio durante bene placito nostro, heredum et successorum nostrorum; quodque de tempore in tempus et ad omnia tempora, post mortem, amotionem, vel sursum redditionem praedicti Henrici, Ducis de Novo Castro, bene liceat et licebit Majori, Aldermannis et Communi Concilio villae praedictae pro tempore existentibus, vel majori parti eorundem (quorum Majorem pro tempore existentem unum esse volumus), unum alium virum discretum et in legibus Angliae peritum eligere et praeficere Recordatorem villae praedictae, continuandum in eodem officio durante bene placito nostro, heredum et successorum nostrorum; et sic toties quoties casus sic acciderit. Et ulterius volumus, ac per praesentes declaramus, quod bene liceat et licebit praedicto Henrico, Duci de Novo Castro, et Recordatori villae praedictae pro tempore existenti, habere, nominare, et facere aliquem alium sufficientem et discretum virum in legibus Angliae eruditum fore et esse Deputatum suum in officio Recordatoris villae praedictae; et quod hujusmodi Deputatus sic factus, nominatus, et juratus habeat et habebit plenam potestatem et authoritatem, in absentia Recordatoris, in omnibus et singulis officio Recordatoris illius spectantibus[1] sive pertinentibus, ad omnes intentiones et proposita quae Recordator villae praedictae pro tempore existens, virtute praesentium seu aliquarum aliarum literarum patentium progenitorum nostrorum in hac parte factarum, habet, aut habere et exercere possit et debet.

Assignavimus etiam, nominavimus, constituimus, et fecimus, ac per praesentes pro nobis, heredibus et successoribus nostris, assignamus, constituimus, nominamus, et facimus dilectum nobis Radolphum Edge, armigerum, fore et esse modernum Communem Clericum villae praedictae, continuandum in eodem officio durante bene placito nostro, heredum et successorum nostrorum; quodque liceat et licebit Majori et Aldermannis villae praedictae pro tempore existentibus, vel majori parti eorundem (quorum Majorem villae praedictae pro tempore existentem unum esse volumus), de tempore in tempus et ad omnia tempora, post mortem, amotionem, vel sursum-redditionem praedicti Radulphi Edge, unum alium discretum et

present Recorder of the town aforesaid, to do and execute all and singular the things that pertain to the office of Recorder in the same town, or in any other town or place incorporated within this our kingdom of England, to continue in the same office during the pleasure of us, our heirs and successors; and that it shall and may be lawful to the Mayor, Aldermen and Common Council of the town aforesaid for the time being, or the greater part of them (of whom we will that the Mayor for the time being shall be one), to elect and advance, from time to time and at all times, after the death, amoval, or surrender of the aforesaid Henry, Duke of Newcastle, one other man discreet and learned in the laws of England to be Recorder of the town aforesaid, to continue in the same office during the pleasure of us, our heirs and successors; and so to do as often as the case shall so happen. And moreover we will, and do declare by these presents, that it may and shall be lawful to the aforesaid Henry, Duke of Newcastle, and to the Recorder of the town aforesaid for the time being to have, name, and make one other sufficient and discreet man learned in the laws of England to be his Deputy in the office of Recorder of the town aforesaid; and that such Deputy so made, named, and sworn, shall and may have full power and authority, in the absence of the Recorder, in all and singular the things pertaining or belonging to the office of such Recorder, for all intents and purposes that the Recorder of the town aforesaid for the time being has, or may or should have and exercise, by virtue of these presents, or of any other letters patent of our progenitors made in this behalf.

CHARLES II.

Power to elect his successor.

The Recorder may appoint a Deputy.

We have also assigned, named, constituted, and made, and do by these presents for us, our heirs and successors, assign, constitute, name, and make our well-beloved Ralph Edge, esquire, to be the present Common Clerk of the town aforesaid, to continue in the same office during the pleasure of us, our heirs and successors; and that it may and shall be lawful to the Mayor and Aldermen of the town aforesaid for the time being, or to the major part of them (of whom we will that the Mayor of the town aforesaid for the time being shall be one) to name, elect, and advance, from time to time and at all times, after the death,

Appointment of Town Clerk.

Power to elect his successor.

---

¹ *spectantibus*,] 'spectand.,' MS.

CHARLES II. honestum virum in officium Communis Clerici pro et in eadem villa nominare, eligere, et praeficere, continuandum in eodem officio durante bene placito nostri, heredum et successorum nostrorum; et sic de tempore in tempus toties quoties casus sic acciderit.

The Recorder and Common Clerk to be approved by the King.

Volumus etiam, et intentionem regiam nostram declaramus, quod nullus Recordator vel Communis Clericus villae praedictae de cetero eligendus sive constituendus intromittat vel intromittant in hujusmodi officio vel officiis, sive eorum alterius respective, antequam approbatus fuerit, vel approbati fuerint, per nos, heredes vel successores nostros, aliquo in praesentibus contento, aut aliqua alia re, causa, vel materia quacunque in contrarium inde in aliquo non obstantibus.

Repetition of Charter of Henry VI.

[1] Et insuper . . . habeantur et teneantur [*as at page 52 above*].

Et quod . . . eligantur [*as at pages 52-54*]. Et quod vicecomites praedicti in forma praedicti eligendi, statim post electionem . . . mittentur [*as at page 54*].

Appointment of Sheriffs.

Et quod Johannes Malyn et Johannes Whitby sint et erunt primi et moderni Vicecomites, continuandi in officio illo usque praedictum festum Sancti Michaëlis Archangeli proximo futurum, et abinde quousque alii electi et praefecti fuerint secundum tenorem et effectum harum literarum patentium nostrarum.

Repetition of Charter of Henry VI.

Et quod tam quilibet Burgensis . . . deberent [*as at pages 54-56*].[2]

Et quod iidem nunc Burgenses . . . intromittat [*as at pages 56-58, with slight alterations*].

Et quod dicti Escaetor . . . certificetur [*as at pages 58-60*].

Concessimus etiam . . . quorumcunque [*as at pages 60-62*].

The Mayor to be an Alderman.

Et ulterius, ex mero motu et certa scientia nostris praedictis, concessimus pro nobis, heredibus et successoribus nostris, praefatis Majori, Aldermannis et Burgensibus dictae villae de Nottingham, ac eorum successoribus imperpetuum, quod praedictus Gervasius Wyld et quilibet succedens Major, postquam ab officio Majoris amotus erit, unus erit, et continuabit unus, ex

---

[1] Here the charter embodies that of Henry VI. with slight alterations of small importance.

[2] The Roll reads after *steterit*, page 56, line 3: 'et nullo tempore Vicecomites ejusdem villae . . . easdem [habeant] potestatem . . . debunt seu debebunt.' The scribe has obviously omitted the four lines that follow *nullo tempore* at p. 56, and has thus merged two separate clauses.

amoval, or surrender of the aforesaid Ralph Edge, one other discreet and honest man to the office of Common Clerk for and in the same town, to continue in the same office during the pleasure of us, our heirs and successors; and so to do from time to time as often as the case shall so happen.

CHARLES II.

We also will, and do declare our royal intention, that no Recorder or Common Clerk of the town aforesaid to be hereafter elected or appointed shall intermeddle in such offices, or either of them respectively, before he or they be approved by us, our heirs or successors, anything in these presents contained, or any other thing, cause, or matter whatsoever to the contrary therein in any wise notwithstanding.

The Recorder and Common Clerk to be approved by the King.

¹And furthermore ... Nottingham by itself for ever [*as at page 53 above*].

Repetition of Charter of Henry VI.

And that the said present Burgesses ... for the year then next to come [*as at pages 53-55*].

And that John Malin and John Whitby may and shall be the first and present Sheriffs, to continue in that office until the aforesaid feast of Saint Michael the Archangel next to come, and from then until two others be elected and advanced according to the tenor and effect of these our letters patent.

Appointment of Sheriffs.

And that as well each Burgess ... within the same our realm [*as at pages 55-57*].³

Repetition of Charter of Henry VI.

And that the same present Burgesses ... except as before excepted [*as at pages 57-59, with slight alterations*].

And that the said Escheator ... of the name of the Escheator of that town [*as at pages 59-61*].

We have also granted ... officers whatsoever [*as at pages 61-63*].

And moreover, of our mere motion and certain knowledge aforesaid, we have granted for us, our heirs and successors, to the aforesaid Mayor, Aldermen and Burgesses of the said town of Nottingham, and to their successors for ever, that the aforesaid Gervase Wild and each succeeding Mayor, after he be amoved from the office of Mayor, shall be, and shall continue to

The Mayor to be an Alderman.

---

³ The Roll reads after 'Mayoralty of that town,' page 57, line 3, above: 'and that at no time hereafter the Sheriffs of the same town ... [shall have] the same power ... within this our realm of England.' The scribe has obviously omitted lines 5 to 7, thus accidentally merging two clauses.

CHARLES II. sex Aldermannis praedictis. Et quod Major et Aldermanni . . . sint Justitiarii nostri . . . qualitercunque in futurum [*as at pages 64-66*].

Concessimus insuper . . . successores suos non obstante [*as at pages 66-70*].

Grant of all lands, liberties, etc., heretofore held by the Burgesses;

Et ulterius, de uberiori gratia nostra speciali, et ex certa scientia et mero motu nostris, concedimus et confirmamus praefatis Majori, Aldermannis et Burgensibus villae praedictae, et successoribus suis, omnia et singula eadem, hujusmodi, et consimilia messuagia, terras, tenementa, et hereditamenta, necnon omnia et singula eadem et hujusmodi libertates, privilegia, franchesias, nundinas, mercata, ferias, fines, amerciamenta, proficua, commoditates, consuetudines, immunitates, quietantias, exemptiones, jura, et jurisdictiones quaecunque, quae Major, Aldermanni et Burgenses villae praedictae, aut aliqui praedecessores sui, per quaecunque nomina, vel per quodcunque nomen, vel per quamcunque incorporationem, vel praetextu cujuscunque incorporationis, modo vel antehac habuerunt, tenuerunt, usi vel gavisi fuerunt, aut habere, tenere, uti vel gaudere debuerunt, habuit, tenuit, usus vel gavisus fuit, debuit aut debuerunt, eis, et successoribus suis, ratione seu praetextu aliquarum cartarum aut literarum patentium aliquorum progenitorum seu antecessorum nostrorum, nuper Regum vel Reginarum Angliae, quoquo modo antehac factarum, confirmatarum, vel concessarum, aut praetextu alicujus praescriptionis, usus, seu consuetudinis, seu quocunque alio legali modo, jure, seu titulo antehac habit-

except the fair of St. Mathias (Feb. 24).

arum, usitatarum, seu consuetarum, excepta una feria ibidem tenta, et teneri consueta, in et super festum Sancti Mathiae Apostoli. Et ulterius volumus, et per praesentes pro nobis,

Grant of two new fairs of eight days each,

heredibus et successoribus nostris, concedimus praefatis Majori, Aldermannis et Burgensibus villae de Nottingham praedictae, et successoribus suis imperpetuum, quod ipsi et successores sui habeant, teneant, et custodiant infra eandem villam, loco praedictae feriae ibidem antehac tentae in et super praedictum festum Sancti Mathiae Apostoli, annuatim imperpetuum quolibet anno duas novas ferias sive nundinas, prima[m] earundem

one beginning April 23, and the other on Nov. 1.

feriarum incipientem in et super vicesimum tertium diem Aprilis quolibet anno, et secunda[m] feria[m] praedictarum feriarum sive nundinarum incipientem in et super primum diem Novembris

be, one of the six Aldermen aforesaid. And that the Mayor and Aldermen ... shall be Justices ... the town and liberty aforesaid [*as at pages 65-67*]. {Charles II.}

We have moreover granted ... their successors [*as at pages 67-71*].

And moreover, of our more ample especial grace, and of our certain knowledge and mere motion, we do grant and confirm to the aforesaid Mayor, Aldermen and Burgesses of the town aforesaid, and to their successors, all and singular the same and the like messuages, lands, tenements, and hereditaments, as well as all and singular the same and such liberties, privileges, franchises, fairs, markets, fairs, fines, amercements, profits, commodities, customs, immunities, acquittances, exemptions, rights, and jurisdictions whatsoever as the Mayor, Aldermen and Burgesses of the town aforesaid, or any of their predecessors, had, held, used, or enjoyed, or ought to have had, held, used, or enjoyed by whatsoever names, or by whatsoever name, or by whatsoever incorporation, or by pretext of whatsoever incorporation, to them, and to their successors, by reason or pretext of any charters or letters patent of any of our progenitors or ancestors, late Kings or Queens of England, in any wise heretofore made, confirmed, or granted, or by pretext of any prescription, use, or custom, or by any other lawful manner, right, or title heretofore had, used, and accustomed, with the exception of a fair held, and accustomed to be held, in and upon the feast of Saint Matthias the Apostle. And moreover we will, and do grant by these presents for us, our heirs and successors, to the aforesaid Mayor, Aldermen and Burgesses of the town of Nottingham aforesaid, and to their successors for ever, that they and their successors shall have, hold, and keep within the same town, in place of the aforesaid fair heretofore held there in and upon the aforesaid feast of Saint Matthias the Apostle, two new fairs annually for ever every year, the first of such fairs beginning in and upon the twenty-third day of April in every year, and the second fair of the aforesaid fairs beginning in and upon the first day of November in every year, unless any of the aforesaid days shall happen to be a Sunday, and then in and upon the Monday next following, and each such fair to endure for eight days; together with a Court of {Grant of all lands, liberties, etc., heretofore held by the Burgesses;} {except the fair of St. Mathias (Feb. 24).} {Grant of two new fairs of eight days each,} {one beginning April 23, and the other on Nov. 1.}

Charles II. quolibet anno, nisi aliquis praedictorum dierum acciderit esse Dies Dominicus, et tunc in et super Diem Lunae proximo sequentem, et quaelibet feria illa per octo dies duratura; unacum Curia Pedis Pulverizati ibidem tempore earundem feriarum et nundinarum respective tenenda, et omnibus libertatibus et liberis consuetudinibus ad hujusmodi Curiam pertinentibus; simul cum tollneto, stallagio, piccagio, finibus, et amerciamentis, ac omnibus aliis proficuis, commoditatibus, et emolumentis de hujusmodi feriis, nundinis, et Curia Pedis Pulverizati provenientibus, incidentibus, emergentibus, seu contingentibus, ac cum omnibus libertatibus et liberis consuetudinibus ad hujusmodi ferias, nundinas, et Curiam Pedis Pulverizati pertinentibus vel spectantibus: ita tamen quod praedictae feriae sive nundinae non sint, seu earum altera, non sit ad nocumentum aliquarum aliarum feriarum sive nundinarum: habenda, tenenda, et gaudenda omnia et singula eadem terras, tenementa, hereditamenta, libertates, privilegia, franchesias, jura, et cetera praemissa eisdem Majori, Aldermannis et Burgensibus villae praedictae, et successoribus suis imperpetuum; reddendo inde nobis, heredibus et successoribus nostris, talia, eadem, hujusmodi, et consimilia reditus, servitia, denariorum summas, et tenuras quae proinde nobis antehac reddiderunt, seu solvere consueverunt et de jure debuerunt.

Grant of liberties, Court of Piepowder, etc., for the said fairs.

Power to enjoy the liberties hereby granted without molestation.

Volumus etiam, et pro nobis, heredibus et successoribus nostris, concedimus praefatis Majori, Aldermannis et Burgensibus villae praedictae, et successoribus suis, per praesentes, quod habeant, teneant, utantur, et gaudeant, et plene habere, tenere, uti, et gaudere possint et valeant imperpetuum omnes libertates, liberas consuetudines, privilegia, authoritates, et quietantias praedictas, secundum tenorem et effectum harum litterarum nostrarum patentium, sine occasione vel impedimento nostri, heredum vel successorum nostrorum quorumcunque; nolentes[1] quod iidem Major, Aldermanni et Burgenses villae praedictae ratione praemissorum, seu eorum alicujus, per nos, vel heredes seu successores nostros, justitiarios, Vicecomites, escaetores, et alios ballivos seu ministros nostros, heredum seu successorum nostrorum quorumcunque, inde occasionentur, molestentur, vexentur, graventur, seu in aliquo perturbentur.

Proviso semper, et volumus ac per praesentes pro nobis,

Piepowder there to be held at the time of the same fairs respectively, and with all liberties and free customs pertaining to such Court; together with toll, stallage, pickage, fines, and amercements, and all other profits, commodities, and emoluments coming from, incidental to, arising, or happening from such fairs and Court of Piepowder, and with all liberties and free customs pertaining or belonging to such fairs and Court of Piepowder: provided that the aforesaid fairs, or either of them, shall not be to the damage of any other fairs: to have, hold, and enjoy all and singular such lands, tenements, hereditaments, liberties, privileges, franchises, rights, and other the premises to the same Mayor, Aldermen and Burgesses of the town aforesaid, and to their successors for ever; rendering therefor to us, our heirs and successors, such, the same, the like, and similar rents, services, sums of money, and tenures as they have heretofore rendered therefor to us, or have been wont to pay and ought of right to pay.

Charles II.

Grant of liberties, Court of Piepowder, etc., for the said fairs.

We also will, and do grant for us, our heirs and successors, by these presents to the aforesaid Mayor, Aldermen and Burgesses of the town aforesaid, and to their successors, that they shall have, hold, use, and enjoy, and may and shall be able to fully have, hold, use, and enjoy for ever all the liberties, free customs, privileges, authorities, and acquittances aforesaid, according to the tenor and effect of these our letters patent, without let or impediment from us, our heirs or successors whatsoever; we being unwilling that the same Mayor, Aldermen and Burgesses of the town aforesaid should be hindered, molested, vexed, aggrieved, or in any wise disturbed therein by reason of the premises, or any of them, by us, or our heirs or successors, justices, Sheriffs, escheators, and other Bailiffs or ministers of us, our heirs or successors whatsoever.

Power to enjoy the liberties hereby granted without molestation.

Provided always, and we will and do by these presents for

---

¹ *nolentes*,] 'volentes,' MS.

CHARLES II.

The Mayor and other officers to take the oaths of Obedience and of Supremacy.

heredibus et successoribus nostris, ordinamus et firmiter injungendo praecipimus, quod Major, Aldermanni, et ceteri omnes officiarii praeantea mentionati et modo constituti sive confirmati, seu constituendi, antequam ipsi ad executionem sive exercitium officii sive officiorum, loci vel locorum, cui vel quibus sic respective nominati, appunctuati, sive constituti modo existunt, aut imposterum nominati, electi, sive constituti fuerint, admittantur, aut aliqualiter in ea parte intromittant, seu eorum aliquis respective intromittat, tam sacramentum corporale communiter vocatum '*The Oath of Obedience*,' quam sacramentum corporale communiter vocatum '*The Oath of Supremacy*' super sacrosanctis Dei Evangeliis praestabunt, et quilibet eorum praestabit, et omnia ad sacramenta, declarationes, et subscriptiones praestabunt et facient, et quilibet eorum praestabit et faciet, qualia per leges et Statuta hujus regni Angliae praestare et facere debent, seu debet, coram tali persona seu talibus personis quales et quae ad hujusmodi sacramenta danda et praestanda et declarationes et subscriptiones recipiendas per legem et Statuta hujus regni nostri Angliae ad praesens appunctuantur et designantur, aut imposterum appunctuatae et designatae fuerit vel fuerint. Et quod praedictus Gervasius Wild, antequam ad officia Majoris, Aldermanni, et Justitiarii Pacis, aut eorum alterius, admittatur, sacramentum suum ad officia illa bene et fideliter exequenda coram praefatis Radulpho Edge, Christophero Hall, Johanne Parker, et Gervasio Rippon, vel aliquibus duobus vel pluribus eorum praestabit: quibus quidem Radulpho Edge, Christophero Hall, Johanni Parker, et Gervasio Rippon administrandi tale sacramentum plenam potestatem et authoritatem damus et concedimus per praesentes.

Power for the Mayor to administer such oaths.

Damus etiam, et per praesentes concedimus, praefatis Gervasio Wyld, et cuilibet succedenti Majori, plenam potestatem et authoritatem sacramenta praestandi omnibus et singulis Aldermannis, Vicecomitibus, et aliis officiariis et Burgensibus villae praedictae modo constitutis, et de cetero imposterum constituendis, ad officia sua respective bene et fideliter exequenda, prout antehac usitatum et consuetum fuerit infra eandem villam ante confectionem harum literarum nostrarum patentium.

Power to make regulations for the

Volumus etiam, ac per praesentes pro nobis, heredibus et successoribus nostris, damus et concedimus Majori, Aldermannis

us, our heirs and successors, ordain and firmly enjoining com- CHARLES II.
mand that the Mayor, Aldermen, and all the other officers
previously mentioned and now constituted or confirmed, or to The Mayor
be constituted, before they be admitted to the execution or and other officers to
exercise of the office or offices, place or places, to which they take the oaths of
are now respectively nominated, appointed, or constituted, or to Obedience
which they shall be hereafter nominated, elected, or constituted, and of Supremacy.
or before they, or any one of them, intermeddle in any wise in
that behalf, shall take, and each of them shall take, as well
the bodily oath commonly called 'the Oath of Obedience,' as
the bodily oath commonly called 'the Oath of Supremacy'
upon God's holy Gospels, and shall make and take, and each
of them shall make and take, all things pertaining to oaths,
declarations, and subscriptions, as by the laws and Statutes
of this kingdom of England they, or he, ought to do and make,
before such person or such persons as are at present appointed
and designated by the law and Statutes of this our realm of
England to give and administer such oaths and to receive
such declarations and subscriptions, or who shall be hereafter
appointed or designated. And that the aforesaid Gervase Wild,
before he be admitted to the offices of Mayor, Alderman, and
Justice of the Peace, or either of them, shall take his oath to
well and faithfully execute those offices before the aforesaid
Ralph Edge, Christopher Hall, John Parker, and Gervase
Rippon, or any two or more of them: to which Ralph Edge,
Christopher Hall, John Parker, and Gervase Rippon we give and
grant by these presents full power and authority to administer
such oath.

We also give, and do by these presents grant to the afore- Power for the
said Gervase Wyld, and to each succeeding Mayor, full power Mayor to administer such
and authority to administer the oaths to all and singular the oaths.
Aldermen, Sheriffs, and others the officers and Burgesses of the
town aforesaid now appointed, and henceforth to be appointed
hereafter, to well and faithfully execute their offices respectively,
as has been hitherto used and accustomed within the same town
before the making of these our letters patent.

We also will, and do give and grant by these presents for us, Power to
our heirs and successors, to the Mayor, Aldermen and Burgesses make regulations for the

CHARLES II.

good of the town.

et Burgensibus villae praedictae, et successoribus suis, quod ipsi et successores sui habeant et habebunt plenam potestatem et authoritatem condendi, constituendi, ordinandi, et stabiliendi de tempore in tempus hujusmodi leges, statuta, jura, ordinationes, et constitutiones rationabiles quaecunque quae eisdem Majori, Aldermannis et Burgensibus villae praedictae, vel majori parti eorum (quorum Majorem pro tempore existentem unum esse volumus), bona, utilia, honesta, et necessaria, juxta eorum sanas discretiones, fore videbuntur pro bono regimine et gubernatione Majoris, Aldermannorum et Burgensium villae praedictae pro tempore existentium, ac omnium officiariorum, ministrorum, artificum, inhabitantium, et residentium infra villam praedictam, libertates et praecinctus ejusdem: proviso semper, quod leges, Statuta, jura, ordinationes, et constitutiones praedicta non sint repugnantia nec contraria legibus hujus regni nostri Angliae.

In cujus rei, etc. Teste Rege apud Westmonasterium, vicesimo octavo die Septembris. Per Breve de Privato Sigillo.

Rot. Litt. Pat., 34 Car. II., pars 7.

XXVI.—*Charter of King James II.*
1688, September 1.

JAMES II.

Appointment of officers.

[1]REX omnibus, ad quos, etc.

Sciatis, quod nos augmentationem [*etc., as at page* 88].[2]

[*George Langford, esquire, created Mayor. The said George Langford, Thomas Smith, John Hawkins, Charles Harvey, Joseph Turpin, Thomas Collins, and John Hides, gentlemen, to be Aldermen.*]

[*John Nevill, John Barrodale, Richard Knight, Robert Marshall, William Burrowes, Joseph James, Thomas Pool, Benjamin Holmes, Abraham Metcalfe, John Crispe, John Welch, Samuel Smith, Joseph Boot, John Huthwait, William Moore, Samuel Rhodes, Roger Hawkesley, and Joseph Sills to be the eighteen Chief Councillors.*]

[1] The original of this charter has not been preserved. It was, like that of Charles II., cancelled by the charter of William and Mary, and was probably then destroyed. It is here printed from the enrolment on the Patent Roll.

[2] From here the charter is practically a repetition of that of Charles II., but the clauses are arranged in different order, and are rendered more concise. Occasionally they are entirely recast. But the differences in intent are so slight, that it is unnecessary to print this charter in full. The differences are of detail, not of con-

of the town aforesaid, and to their successors, that they and their successors shall and may have full power and authority to make, constitute, ordain, and establish from time to time such reasonable laws, statutes, rights, ordinances, and constitutions whatsoever as shall seem to the same Mayor, Aldermen and Burgesses of the town aforesaid, or to the major part of them (of whom we will that the Mayor for the time being shall be one), according to their sound discretions, to be good, useful, honest, and necessary for the good rule and government of the Mayor, Aldermen and Burgesses of the town aforesaid for the time being, and of all the officers, ministers, artificers, inhabitants, and residents within the town aforesaid, the liberties and precincts of the same: provided always that the laws, Statutes, rights, ordinances, and constitutions aforesaid shall not be repugnant nor contrary to the laws of this our kingdom of England.

Charles II. Good of the town.

In witness whereof, etc. Witness the King at Westminster, the twenty-eighth day of September. By Writ of Privy Seal.

Patent Roll, 34 Charles II., part 7.

XXVI.—*Charter of King James II.*
1688, September 1.

¹ The King to all to whom, etc.

Know ye that we desiring [*etc., as at page* 89].²

James II.

[*George Langford, esquire, created Mayor. The said George Langford, Thomas Smith, John Hawkins, Charles Harvey, Joseph Turpin, Thomas Collins, and John Hides, gentlemen, to be Aldermen.*]

Appointment of officers.

[*John Nevill, John Barrodale, Richard Knight, Robert Marshall, William Burrows, Joseph James, Thomas Pool, Benjamin Holmes, Abraham Metcalfe, John Crisp, John Welch, Samuel Smith, Joseph Boot, John Huthwait, William Moore, Samuel Rhodes, Roger Hawkesley, and Joseph Sills to be the eighteen Chief Councillors.*]

stitution. The only important change is the addition to the provisoes for the amoval of the various officers of the Corporation of the clause *vel modo et forma inferius mentionata* (*i.e.,* unless they be amoved for the reasons stated in the Charter of Charles II., 'or in the manner and form below mentioned'). The reference is to the power reserved in this charter to the King to remove any of the officers of the Corporation.

JAMES II.

[*William Cockle, Caleb Wilkinson, William Orme, William Baines, William Bellfin, and John France to be Councillors.*]
[*Thomas Cooke and Samuel Watkinson to be Chamberlains.*]
[*Henry, Duke of Newcastle, to be Recorder.*]
[*Charles Bawdes, esquire, to be Common Clerk.*]
[*John Nevill and John Borradale to be Coroners.*]
[*Joseph Boot and John Huthwaite to be Sheriffs.*]

Abolition of the two fairs granted by Charles II.

[*Grant of all rights, immunities, lands, tenements, etc., heretofore held by the Mayor and Burgesses*] exceptis duabus feriis per praecharissimum fratrem nostrum Dominum Carolum Secundum, nuper Regem Angliae, per literas suas patentes sub magno sigillo Angliae confectas, gerentes datum 'vicesimo octavo die Septembris, anno regni' sui 'tricesimo quarto,' nuper Majori, Aldermannis et Burgensibus villae praedictae, et successoribus suis, concessis, tenendis apud villam praedictam in et super vicesimum tertium diem Aprilis et primum diem Novembris in quolibet anno, et per septem dies post quemlibet dierum praedictorum; quas quidem duas ferias exnunc abolendas ordinamus

Grant of two other fairs,

et constituimus; et in loco praedictarum feriarum, damus et per praesentes pro nobis, heredibus et successoribus nostris, concedimus modo Majori, Aldermannis et Burgensibus villae praedictae, et successoribus suis imperpetuum, duas alias ferias sive nundinas apud villam praedictam annuatim tenendas, videlicet,

Sept. 21.

unam feriam sive nundinam in festo Sancti Mathaei Apostoli et per septem dies dictum festum immediate sequentes, et alteram

Feb. 24.

feriarum sive nundinarum in festo Sancti Matthiae Apostoli et per septem dies dictum festum immediate sequentes quolibet anno imperpetuum. [*Grant of Court of Piepowder, of tolls, etc., during the same fairs.*]

Power reserved to the King to amove any officer.

Proviso semper, ac plenam potestatem et authoritatem nobis, heredibus et successoribus nostris, per praesentes reservamus, de tempore in tempus et ad omnia tempora imposterum, ad Majorem, Recordatorem, Communem Clericum, aliquem vel aliquos de Aldermannis, Capitalibus Conciliariis, Conciliariis, Coronatoribus, Vicecomitibus, et Camerariis villae praedictae pro tempore existentibus ad libitum vel beneplacitum nostrum, heredum et successorum nostrorum, per aliquem ordinem nostrum, sive heredum vel successorum nostrorum, in Privato Concilio factum et sub sigillo Privati Concilii praedicti eisdem

[*William Cockle, Caleb Wilkinson, William Orme, William* JAMES II.
Baines, William Bellfin, and John France to be Councillors.]
  [*Thomas Cooke and Samuel Watkinson to be Chamberlains.*]
  [*Henry, Duke of Newcastle, to be Recorder.*]
  [*Charles Bawdes, esquire, to be Common Clerk.*]
  [*John Nevill and John Borradale to be Coroners.*]
  [*Joseph Boot and John Huthwait to be Sheriffs.*]

  [*Grant of all rights, immunities, lands, tenements, etc., hereto-* Abolition of
fore held by the Mayor and Burgesses] excepting two fairs granted by
granted by our very dear brother the Lord Charles the Second, Charles II.
late King of England, by his letters patent made under the
great seal of England, bearing date 'the twenty-eighth day of
September, in the thirty-fourth year of' his 'reign,' to the late
Mayor, Aldermen and Burgesses of the town aforesaid, and
their successors, to be held at the town aforesaid in and upon
the twenty-third day of April and the first day of November in
each year, and for seven days after each of the aforesaid days;
which two fairs we ordain and appoint to be henceforth
abolished; and in place of the aforesaid fairs, we give and do by Grant of two
these presents grant for us, our heirs and successors, to the other fairs,
present Mayor, Aldermen and Burgesses of the town aforesaid,
and to their successors for ever, two other fairs to be held
annually at the town aforesaid, to wit, one fair in the feast of
Saint Matthew the Apostle and for seven days immediately Sept. 21.
following the said feast, and another fair in the feast of Saint
Matthias the Apostle and for seven days immediately following Feb. 24.
the said feast every year for ever. [*Grant of Court of Piepowder,
of tolls, etc., during the same fairs.*]

Provided always, and by these presents we do reserve full Power re-
power and authority to us, our heirs and successors, from time King to
to time and at all times hereafter, to amove, and declare to be amove any
amoved, the Mayor, Recorder, Common Clerk, any one or more officer.
of the Aldermen, Chief Councillors, Councillors, Coroners,
Sheriffs, and Chamberlains of the town aforesaid for the time
being at the will or pleasure of us, our heirs and successors, by
any order of us or our heirs or successors, made in the Privy
Council and signified under the seal of the Privy Council aforesaid to them respectively; and as often as we, our heirs or
successors, shall declare, by any such order made in Privy

JAMES II.

respective significatum, amovendos et amotum et amotos esse declarandos; et quoties nos, heredes vel successores nostri, per aliquem talem ordinem in Privato Concilio factum declarabimus hujusmodi Majorem, Recordatorem, Communem Clericum, aliquem vel aliquos de Aldermannis, Capitalibus Conciliariis, Conciliariis, Coronatoribus, Vicecomitibus, et Camerariis villae praedictae pro tempore existentibus, seu eorum aliquem vel aliquos, fore et esse amotum et amotos a respectivis officiis suis, quod tunc et extunc Major, Recordator, Communis Clericus, Aldermannus vel Aldermanni, Capitales Conciliarii, Concilarii, Coronatores, Vicecomites, et Camerarii villae praedictae pro tempore existentes sic amotum vel amotos esse declarati, vel declarandi, a separalibus et respectivis officiis suis ipso facto et sine ullo ulteriori processu realiter et ad omnia intentiones et proposita quaecunque amoti sint et erunt,[1] et amotus sit et erit; et hoc quoties casus sic acciderit, aliquo in contrarium inde non obstante; ac adtunc et in tali casu, infra conveniens tempus post hujusmodi amotionem vel amotiones, alia idonea persona vel idoneae personae in locum et officium, sive loca respectiva vel officia, hujusmodi personae vel personarum sic amotae vel amotarum eligetur et constituetur, eligentur et constituentur, et eligi et constitui possit et possint, secundum tenorem et appunctuationem harum literarum patentium.

Power reserved to the King to appoint successors to any officers.

Volumus etiam, quod si aliquando imposterum, infra viginti dies post hujusmodi amotionem vel amotiones Majoris, Recordatoris, Aldermannorum, Capitalium Conciliariorum, Conciliariorum, Coronatorum, Vicecomitum, et Camerariorum villae praedictae pro tempore existentium, alicujus vel aliquorum eorum, ab officiis suis respectivis, aut post mortem eorundem, vel aliquorum eorum, nos, heredes vel successores nostri, per literas mandatorias sub sigillo vel signeto manuali nostro, heredum vel successorum nostrorum, Majori, Aldermannis et Burgensibus villae praedictae pro temporibus existentibus, vel aliquibus eorum, praeceperimus eligere et admittere et jurare aliquam vel aliquas personas in eisdem literis mandatoriis nominatas ad et in separalia respectiva officia et loca, officium vel locum, alicujus personae vel personarum sic amotae vel amotarum, quod tunc et toties quaelibet persona sic nominata in talibus literis mandatoriis eligetur, admittetur, et juretur in

Council, such Mayor, Recorder, Common Clerk, any one or more of the Aldermen, Chief Councillors, Councillors, Coroners, Sheriffs, and Chamberlains of the town aforesaid for the time being, or any one or more of them, to be amoved from their respective offices, that then and thereupon the Mayor, Recorder, Common Clerk, Alderman or Aldermen, Chief Councillors, Councillors, Coroners, Sheriffs, and Chamberlains of the town aforesaid for the time being so declared, or to be declared, to be amoved, may and shall be *ipso facto* and without any further process really and for all intents and purposes whatsoever amoved, and each of them shall be amoved, from their several and respective offices; and this so often as the case shall so happen, anything to the contrary thereof notwithstanding; and that then and in such case, within a convenient time after such amoval or amovals, another fitting person or other fitting persons shall be elected and appointed, and may be elected and appointed, according to the tenor and appointment of these letters patent, to the place and office, or respective places or offices, of such person or persons so amoved.

We also will, that if at any time hereafter, within twenty days after such amoval or amovals of the Mayor, Recorder, Aldermen, Chief Councillors, Councillors, Coroners, Sheriffs, and Chamberlains of the town aforesaid for the time being, any one or more of them, from their respective offices, or after their death, or the death of any of them, we, our heirs or successors, shall, by letters mandatory under the seal or signet of us, our heirs and successors, enjoin the Mayor, Aldermen and Burgesses of the town aforesaid for the time being, or any of them, to elect and admit and swear any person or persons named in the same letters mandatory to and in the several respective offices and places, office and place, of any person or persons so amoved, then and so often each person so named in such letters mandatory shall be elected, admitted, and sworn to the place or office within the town aforesaid in or to which he shall be

Power reserved to the King to appoint successors to any officers.

¹ *erunt*,] 'erint,' MS.

JAMES II.

locum sive officium in villa praedicta in vel ad quod per tales literas mandatorias nostras nominata et appunctuata erit; et quod quaelibet electio sive admissio habenda contra tenorem harum praesentium aut contra exigentiam talium literarum patentium vacua et nullius vigoris erit.

Exemption of officers from taking various oaths, the Sacrament, etc.

[*Grant to the officers above named and their successors of exemption from taking the Oaths of Supremacy and of Allegiance or Obedience, the oath prescribed in the Statute 13 Charles II., entitled 'An Act for the well governing and regulating of Corporacions,' and from receiving the Sacrament of the Lord's Supper according to the rites of the Church of England or the directions*

13 Car. II., Stat. II., c. 1.

of any Canons or Statutes of the realm of England, and from taking and subscribing the declarations contained in the above Statute of 13 Charles II.; and from subscribing the declarations

25 Car. II., c. 2.

contained in the Statute 25 Charles II. entitled 'An Act for preventing dangers which may happen from Popish Recusants;' and from all oaths, declarations, etc., contained or mentioned in the said Statutes; and from all pains and penalties incurred by their not taking such oaths, declarations, etc. They are also granted full power to exercise their offices without taking such oaths, declarations, sacrament, etc., as fully as if they had taken them.]

No Recorder or Common Clerk to be admitted to his office until he has been approved by the King.

Volumus denique, ac per praesentes pro nobis, heredibus et successoribus nostris, ordinamus et declaramus, quod nullus Recordator vel Communis Clericus villae praedictae de cetero eligendus sive constituendus ad executionem officii sui respective admittatur, nisi approbatio et consensus noster, heredum vel successorum nostrorum, sub sigillo et signeto manuali nostro, ac heredum vel successorum nostrorum, in ea parte prius significabitur, aliquo in praesentibus contento aut aliqua alia re, causa, vel materia quacunque in contrarium non obstante.

In cujus, etc. Teste Rege, apud Westmonasterium, primo die Septembris.   Per ipsum Regem.

Rot. Litt. Patent., 4 Jac. II., pars 18, m. 17.

XXVII.—*Charter of William and Mary.*
1692, October 19.

WILLIAM AND MARY.

GULIELMUS et MARIA, Dei gratia, Angliae, Scotiae, Franciae, et Hiberniae Rex et Regina, Fidei Defensores, etc., omnibus, ad quos praesentes literae nostrae pervenerint, salutem.

named and appointed by such our letters mandatory; and that every election or admission to be had against the tenor of these presents or against the demand of such letters patent shall be void and of no force.

[*Grant to the officers above named and their successors of exemption from taking the Oaths of Supremacy and of Allegiance or Obedience, the oath prescribed in the Statute* 13 *Charles II., entitled* '*An Act for the well governing and regulating of Corporacions,*' *and from receiving the Sacrament of the Lord's Supper according to the rites of the Church of England or the directions of any Canons or Statutes of the realm of England, and from taking and subscribing the declarations contained in the above Statute of* 13 *Charles II.; and from subscribing the declarations contained in the Statute* 25 *Charles II. entitled* '*An Act for preventing dangers which may happen from Popish Recusants;*' *and from all oaths, declarations, etc., contained or mentioned in the said Statutes; and from all pains and penalties incurred by their not taking such oaths, declarations, etc. They are also granted full power to exercise their offices without taking such oaths, declarations, sacrament, etc., as fully as if they had taken them.*]

JAMES II.

Exemption of officers from taking various oaths, the Sacrament, etc.

13 Car. II., Stat. II., c. 1.

25 Car. II., c. 2.

We will finally, and do by these presents for us, our heirs and successors, ordain and declare that no Recorder or Common Clerk of the town aforesaid to be hereafter elected or appointed shall be respectively admitted to the execution of their office, unless the approval and consent of us, our heirs or successors, in that behalf shall be first signified under the seal and sign manual of us, and our heirs or successors, anything in these presents contained or any other thing, cause, or matter to the contrary notwithstanding.

No Recorder or Common Clerk to be admitted to his office until he has been approved by the King.

In witness, etc. Witness the King, at Westminster, the first day of September. By the King himself.

Patent Roll, 4 James II., part 18, m. 17.

XXVII.—*Charter of William and Mary.*
1692, October 19.

WILLIAM and MARY, by the grace of God, of England, Scotland, France, and Ireland King and Queen, Defenders of the Faith, etc., to all to whom our present letters shall come, greeting.

WILLIAM AND MARY.

I

WILLIAM AND MARY.

Recital of *Inspeximus* of James I.

Confirmation of preceding charters.

For the removal of the doubts that have arisen owing to the pretended surrender of the charters,

Inspeximus quasdam literas patentes sub magno sigillo Angliae gerentes datum apud Westmonasterium, duodecimo die Februarii, anno regni nuper Regis Jacobi Angliae, Franciae, et Hiberniae vicesimo et Scotiae quinquagesimo sexto factas et concessas Majori et Burgensibus villae Notyngham in haec verba: 'JACOBUS, Dei gratia' [*etc., reciting exemplification by James I. of Charter of Henry VI., No. XXIII.*].

Nos autem omnia et singula franchesias, libertates, privilegia, quietantias, immunitates, concessiones, confirmationes, et restitutiones praedicta rata habentes et grata,[1] [ea] pro nobis, heredibus et successoribus nostris, quantum in nobis est, acceptamus, approbamus, et ratificamus, ac omnia et singula franchesias, libertates, privilegia, quietantias, et immunitates praedicta dilectis nobis Majori et Burgensibus villae praedictae, et successoribus suis, tenore praesentium concedimus et confirmamus, sicut cartae praedictae rationabiliter testantur, et prout iidem Major et Burgenses ejusdem villae Notyngham, vel praedecessores sui, unquam franchesiis, libertatibus, privilegiis, quietantiis, et immunitatibus praedictis uti et gaudere debent, potuerunt, seu debuerunt, licet dicti Major et Burgenses ejusdem villae vel praedecessores sui franchesiis, libertatibus, privilegiis, quietantiis, et immunitatibus praedictis, seu eorum aliquo vel aliquibus abusi vel non usi fuerint.

Cumque datum est nobis intelligi, quod, praetextu cujusdam instrumenti vel scripti ad quod Commune Sigillum Majoris et Burgensium villae praedictae combinatione[2] paucorum ejusdem villae appositum et affixum fuerat, gerentis datum decimo octavo die Septembris, anno regni Domini Caroli Secundi nuper Regis, antecessoris nostri, felicis memoriae tricesimo[3] quarto, et in Curia Cancellariae ejusdem nuper Regis de recordo irrotulati, purportantis fore concessionem per praefatos Majorem et Burgenses eidem nuper Regi, heredibus et successoribus suis, de omnibus et singulis maneriis, messuagiis, terris, tenementis, redditibus, et hereditamentis, cum pertinentiis quibuscunque, de, vel in, quibus dicti Major et Burgenses ad tunc vel ad aliquod tempus ante tunc fuerunt aliquo modo seisiti, possessionati, vel interessati in jure incorporationis suae vel capacitate sua incorporata aliquibus modis quibuscunque, ac etiam purportantis fore

[1] *grata,*] 'gratia,' MS. [2] *combinatione,*] 'combinationem,' MS.

We have inspected certain letters patent under the great seal of England bearing date at Westminster, the twelfth day of February, in the years of the reign of the late King James of England, France, and Ireland the twentieth and of Scotland the fifty-sixth, made and granted to the Mayor and Burgesses of the town of Nottingham in these words: 'JAMES, by the grace of God' [*etc., reciting exemplification by James I. of Charter of Henry VI., No. XXIII.*]. WILLIAM AND MARY.
Recital of *Inspeximus* of James I.

We, esteeming all and singular the franchises, liberties, privileges, acquittances, immunities, grants, confirmations, and restitutions aforesaid as valid and acceptable, do, for us, our heirs and successors, so far as in us lies, accept, approve, and ratify them, and do grant and confirm by the tenor of these presents all and singular the franchises, liberties, privileges, acquittances, and immunities aforesaid to our well-beloved the Mayor and Burgesses of the town aforesaid, and to their successors, as the charters aforesaid do reasonably testify, and as the same Mayor and Burgesses of the same town of Nottingham, or their predecessors, at any time ought to have, might, or should have used and enjoyed the franchises, liberties, privileges, acquittances, and immunities aforesaid, although the said Mayor and Burgesses of the same town, or their predecessors, have misused or not used the franchises, liberties, privileges, acquittances, and immunities aforesaid. Confirmation of preceding charters.

And whereas we are given to understand that, under pretext of a certain instrument or writing to which the Common Seal of the Mayor and Burgesses of the town aforesaid had been placed and affixed by a combination of a few men of the same town, bearing date the eighteenth day of September, in the thirty-fourth year of the reign of the Lord Charles the Second late King, our predecessor, of happy memory, and enrolled of record in the Court of Chancery of the same late King, purporting to be a gift by the aforesaid Mayor and Burgesses to the said late King, his heirs and successors, of all and singular the manors, messuages, lands, tenements, rents, and hereditaments, with their appurtenances whatsoever, of, or in, which the said Mayor and Burgesses at that time or at any time before then were in any wise seized, possessed, or interested in right of For the removal of the doubts that have arisen owing to the pretended surrender of the charters,

³ *tricesimo*,] 'tricessimo,' MS. So occasionally.

WILLIAM AND MARY.
concessionem et sursum redditionem per praefatos Majorem et Burgenses eidem nuper Regi de omnibus franchesiis, chartis, literis patentibus incorporationis, potestatibus, libertatibus, et immunitatibus quibuscunque ad aliquod tempus vel tempora concessis ad, vel gavisis per, eosdem Majorem et Burgenses vel praedecessores suos, vel aliquos eorum, aliquibus viis aut

and to the Charters of Charles II. & James II.,
modis vel per aliquod nomen sive nomina quaecunque; nec non quod, tam ratione praedictae praetensae concessionis et sursum redditionis, quam praetextu seu colore diversarum cartarum sive literarum patentium incorporationis praedictarum per nuper Regem Carolum Secundum ac per Jacobum Secundum nuper Regem factarum et concessarum, seu mentionatarum fore concessarum, post datum dicti instrumenti vel praetensae sursum redditionis, diversa dubia, quaestiones, et controversiae orta fuerunt de, et concernentia, libertatibus, franchesiis, et consuetudinibus, terris, et possessionibus Majoris et Burgensium villae praedictae, ac etiam de, et concernentia, electione et continuatione quorundam officiariorum villae praedictae.

we appoint William Greaves, the Mayor at the time of the pretended surrender, to be Mayor.
Sciatis igitur, quod nos pacem, tranquilitatem, et bonam gubernationem ejusdem villae et Burgensium et inhabitantium ejusdem gratiose affectantes, et omnia dicta dubia, quaestiones, et controversias in hac parte auferre designantes, de gratia nostra speciali ac ex certa scientia et mero motu nostris, de advisamento Privati Concilii nostri, assignavimus, nominavimus, ordinavimus, constituimus, et confirmavimus, ac per praesentes pro nobis, heredibus et successoribus nostris, assignamus, nominamus, ordinamus, constituimus, et confirmamus Willelmum Greaves, generosum, qui fuit Major villae Notyngham praedictae tempore ejusdem praetensae sursum redditionis, fore et esse praesentem et modernum Majorem villae praedictae, continuandum in eodem officio a data praesentium usque ad usuale tempus pro electione Majoris pro eadem villa in festo Sancti Michaëlis Archangeli, quod erit anno Domini millesimo sexcentesimo nonagesimo tertio, si dictus Willelmus Greaves tam diu vixerit.

Grant of power to appoint 18 Common Councillors
Et ulterius volumus, ac per praesentes pro nobis, heredibus vel successoribus nostris, Majori et Burgensibus villae praedictae, et successoribus suis, concedimus potestatem et authoritatem, ad aliquod sive aliqua tempus seu tempora infra spatium duorum

their incorporation or in their corporate capacity by any means whatsoever, and also purporting to be a gift and surrender by the aforesaid Mayor and Burgesses to the said late King of all franchises, charters, letters patent of incorporation, powers, liberties, and immunities whatsoever granted at any time or times to, or enjoyed by, the same Mayor and Burgesses, or their predecessors, or any of them, in any means or ways or by any name or names whatsoever; and also that, as well by reason of the aforesaid pretended grant and surrender as under pretext or colour of divers charters or letters patent of incorporation aforesaid made and granted, or mentioned as being granted, by the late King Charles the Second and by James the Second late King after the date of the said instrument or pretended surrender, divers doubts, questions, and controversies have arisen of and concerning the liberties, franchises, and customs, the lands and possessions of the Mayor and Burgesses of the town aforesaid, and also of and concerning the election and continuation of certain officers of the town aforesaid.

_{WILLIAM AND MARY.}

_{and to the Charters of Charles II. & James II.,}

Know ye therefore, that we, graciously considering the peace, tranquility, and good government of the same town and of the Burgesses and inhabitants of the same, and designing to settle all the said doubts, questions, and controversies in this behalf, have, of our especial grace and of our certain knowledge and mere motion, with the advice of our Privy Council, assigned, nominated, ordained, created, and confirmed, and do by these presents for ourselves, our heirs and successors, assign, name, ordain, create, and confirm William Greaves, gentleman, who was Mayor of the town of Nottingham aforesaid at the time of the same pretended surrender, to be the present and modern Mayor of the town aforesaid, to continue in the same office from the date of these presents until the usual time for the election of a Mayor for the same town at the feast of Saint Michael the Archangel, which will be in the year of our Lord one thousand, six hundred and ninety-three, if the said William Greaves live so long.

_{we appoint William Greaves, the Mayor at the time of the pretended surrender, to be Mayor.}

And moreover we will, and by these presents for ourselves, our heirs and successors, do grant power and authority to the Mayor and Burgesses of the town aforesaid, and their successors, to elect, nominate, and appoint, at any time or times within the

_{Grant of power to appoint 18 Common Councillors}

WILLIAM AND MARY.

as before the pretended surrender.

mensium proximo post datum praesentium, eligere, nominare, et constituere aliquos Burgenses ejusdem villae ad officium de Communi Concilio villae praedictae, ac fore et esse de Communi Concilio ejusdem villae, tam ex iis qui officium Vicecomitis villae praedictae servierunt sive habuerunt, quam qui officium illud non servierunt vel habuerunt, quos Majori et Burgensibus villae praedictae, vel majori parti eorum, melius expedire videbitur, ad complendum numerum octodecim de Communi Concilio villae praedictae, toties quoties necesse fuerit infra dictum spatium duorum mensium proximo post datum praesentium. Et ulterius volumus, ac per praesentes pro nobis, heredibus et successoribus nostris, concedimus et confirmamus Majori et Burgensibus villae praedictae, et successoribus suis, quod, post hujusmodi electionem et expirationem duorum mensium praedictorum proximo post datum praesentium, ut praefertur, liceat et licebit Majori et Burgensibus villae praedictae, et successoribus suis, de tempore in tempus ad omnia tempora imperpetuum eligere, nominare, et constitu[e]re idoneas personas ad officium de Communi Concilio villae praedictae, et fore et esse de Communi Concilio ejusdem villae, in tali modo et forma prout in eadem villa assuetum et consuetum fuit ante diem datus praedictae praetensae sursum redditionis, videlicet, praedictum decimum octavum diem Septembris, anno regni dicti nuper Regis Caroli Secundi tricesimo quarto, vel ad aliquod tempus praeantea: proviso semper, et volumus, quod dictus Willelmus Greaves, antequam ad executionem officii Majoris villae praedictae admittatur, praestabit sacramentum suum corporale pro debita executione officii Majoris villae praedictae ac etiam sacramenta per quendam Actum in Parliamento nostro apud Westmonasterium anno regni nostri primo tento editum et provisum appunctuata fore capta et praestita, coram Thoma Trigg et Radulpho Bennett, generosis, aut altero eorum: quibus Thomae Trigg et Radulpho Bennett, vel alteri eorum, dicta separalia[1] sacramenta administrandi plenam potestatem et authoritatem damus et concedimus per praesentes.

The Mayor to take oaths before he enters office.

1 W. & M., c. 8.

Pardon of offences committed since the pretended surrender.

Et de uberiori gratia nostra speciali, et ex certa scientia et mero motu nostris, pardonavimus, remisimus, et relaxavimus, ac per praesentes pro nobis, heredibus et successoribus nostris, pardonamus, remittimus, et relaxamus Majori et Burgensibus

space of two months next after the date of these presents, any Burgesses of the same town to the office of the Common Council of the town aforesaid, and to be of the Common Council of the same town, as well from those who have served or held the office of Sheriff of the town aforesaid, as from those who have not served or do not hold that office, whom the Mayor and Burgesses of the town aforesaid, or the major part of them, shall deem most fit, to fulfil the number of eighteen of the Common Council of the town aforesaid, as many times as shall be necessary, within the said space of two months next after the date of these presents. And moreover we will, and do by these presents for ourselves, our heirs and successors, grant and confirm to the Mayor and Burgesses of the town aforesaid, and their successors, that, after such election and the expiration of the two months aforesaid next after the date of these presents, as is aforesaid, it may and shall be lawful to the Mayor and Burgesses of the town aforesaid, and to their successors, from time to time at all times for ever to elect, name, and appoint fit persons to the office of Common Council of the town aforesaid, and to be of the Common Council of the same town, in such manner and form as was used and accustomed in the same town before the day of the date of the aforesaid pretended surrender, to wit, the aforesaid eighteenth day of September, in the thirty-fourth year of the reign of the said late King Charles the Second, or at any time before then: provided always, and we will, that the said William Greaves shall, before he be admitted to the execution of the office of Mayor of the town aforesaid, take his bodily oath for the due execution of the office of Mayor of the town aforesaid and also the oaths appointed to be taken and sworn by an Act issued and provided in our Parliament holden at Westminster in the first year of our reign, before Thomas Trigg and Ralph Bennett, gentlemen, or either of them; to which Thomas Trigg and Ralph Bennett, or either of them, we give and grant by these presents full power and authority to administer the said several oaths.

WILLIAM AND MARY.

as before the pretended surrender.

The Mayor to take oaths before he enters office.

1 W. & M., c. 8.

And of our more ample especial grace, and of our certain knowledge and mere motion, we have pardoned, remitted, and released, and do by these presents for ourselves, our heirs and

Pardon of offences committed since the pretended surrender,

¹ *separalia*,] 'seperalia,' MS.

WILLIAM AND MARY.

and in consequence of the Charters of Charles II. and James II.

villae praedictae omnia et singula res, materias, contemptus, crimina, et offensas et transgressiones quaecunque per se ipsos facta, commissa, sive perpetrata de, pro, in, vel concernentia, executione vel non-executione aut mala executione aliquorum officiorum infra villam praedictam, limites, vel praecinctus ejusdem ad aliquod tempus sive tempora post praedictum decimum octavum diem Septembris, anno dicti nuper Regis Caroli Secundi tricesimo quarto supra-dicto; ac etiam pardonavimus, remisimus, et relaxavimus, ac per praesentes pro nobis, et heredibus et successoribus nostris, pardonamus, remittimus, et relaxamus omnibus et singulis Burgensibus villae de Notyngham praedicta omnia et singula res, materias, contemptus, crimina, offensas, et transgressiones quaecunque per se ipsos vel aliquem sive aliquos eorum separatim¹ vel conjunctim facta, commissa, sive perpetrata de, pro, vel in executione alicujus officii vel aliquorum officiorum infra villam praedictam, limites vel praecinctus ejusdem, colore sive praetextu aliquarum literarum patentium praedictorum nuper Regum Caroli Secundi et Jacobi Secundi, vel alterius eorum, ad aliquod tempus sive tempora post praedictum decimum octavum diem Septembris, anno dicti nuper Regis Caroli Secundi tricesimo quarto supra-dicto.

Restitution of all liberties, lands, etc., held by the Burgesses in the time of James I.,

Et ulterius, de uberiori gratia nostra speciali, ac ex certa scientia et mero motu nostris, dedimus, concessimus, restituimus, confirmavimus, approbavimus, et ratificavimus, ac per praesentes pro nobis, heredibus et successoribus nostris, damus, concedimus, restituimus, confirmamus, approbamus, et ratificamus Majori et Burgensibus villae Notyngham, et successoribus suis, omnia et omnimoda manneria, messuagia, molendina, redditus, terras, tenementa, decimas, prata, pascua, pasturas, communias, ferias, nundinas, mercata, et tot, tanta, talia, eadem, et hujusmodi potestates, praescriptiones, libertates, privilegia, franchesias, immunitates, jurisdictiones, chartas, literas patentes, literas patentes incorporationis, consuetudines, proficua, officia, officiarios, exemptiones, quietantias, vasta, vacua funda, commoditates, emolumenta, bona, catalla, et hereditamenta quaecunque quot, quanta, qualia, et quae per dictas literas patentes gerentes datum dicto duodecimo die Februarii, anno regni dicti Regis Jacobi Primi Angliae, Franchiae, et Hiberniae vicesimo et Scotiae quinquagesimo sexto, concessa et confirmata fuerunt, vel

successors, pardon, remit, and release to the Mayor and Burgesses of the town aforesaid all and singular things, matters, contempts, crimes, and offences and trespasses whatsoever by them made, committed, or done of, for, in, or concerning the execution or non-execution or bad execution of any offices within the town aforesaid, the limits, or precincts of the same at any time or times after the aforesaid eighteenth day of September, in the abovesaid thirty-fourth year of the said late King Charles the Second ; and we have also pardoned, remitted, and released, and by these presents do for ourselves, and our heirs and successors, pardon, remit, and release to all and singular the Burgesses of the town of Nottingham aforesaid all and singular things, matters, contempts, crimes, offences, and trespasses whatsoever made, committed, or done by them or by any of them severally or jointly of, for, or in execution of any office or of any offices within the town aforesaid, the limits or precincts of the same, by colour or pretext of any letters patent of the aforesaid late Kings Charles the Second and James the Second, or of either of them, at any time or times after the aforesaid eighteenth day of September, in the abovesaid thirty-fourth year of the said late King Charles the Second.

WILLIAM AND MARY.

and in consequence of the Charters of Charles II. and James II.

And moreover, of our more especial grace, and of our certain knowledge and mere motion, we have given, granted, restored, confirmed, approved, and ratified, and by these presents do for ourselves, our heirs and successors, give, grant, restore, confirm, approve, and ratify to the Mayor and Burgesses of the town of Nottingham, and to their successors, all and all manner the manors, messuages, mills, rents, lands, tenements, tithes, meadows, pastures, pasture-lands, commons, fairs, markets, and such, so many, the same, and the like powers, prescriptions, liberties, privileges, franchises, immunities, jurisdictions, charters, letters patent, letters patent of incorporation, customs, profits, offices, officers, exemptions, acquittances, wastes, waste grounds, commodities, emoluments, goods, chattels, and hereditaments whatsoever as were granted and confirmed, or mentioned to be granted and confirmed, by the said letters patent bearing date the said twelfth day of February, in the year of the reign of the said King James the First of England, France, and Ireland the

Restitution of all liberties, lands, etc., held by the Burgesses in the time of James I.,

---

² *separatim*,] 'seperatim,' MS.

WILLIAM AND MARY.

or that they had before the pretended surrender.

mentionata fore concessa et confirmata, aut per aliquas alias praedictas literas patentes concessa, seu mentionata fore concessa aut confirmata, Majori et Burgensibus villae praedictae, sive quae Major et Burgenses villae praedictae, vel praedecessores sui, per quodcunque nomen seu quaecunque nomina incorporationis, ante dictum decimum octavum diem Septembris, anno regni dicti nuper Regis Caroli Secundi tricesimo quarto supra-dicto, habuerunt, tenuerunt, usi vel gavisi fuerunt, aut occupaverunt, aut habere, tenere, uti vel gaudere debuerunt aut potuerunt sibi et successoribus suis, ratione aut praetextu praedictarum separalium[1] literarum patentium, vel earum aliquarum vel alicujus, vel aliarum cartarum, concessionum, aut literarum patentium quarumcunque per aliquem progenitorum aut antecessorum nostrorum nuper Regum vel Reginarum Angliae quoquomodo factarum, concessarum, seu confirmatarum ante dictum decimum octavum diem Septembris, anno regni dicti nuper Regis Caroli Secundi tricesimo quarto, aut quocunque alio legali modo, jure, sive titulo, consuetudine, usu, sive praescriptione ante datum praesentium legitime usitata, habita, consueta, sive gavisa.

Confirmation of demises, etc., made by the pretended Council created after the pretended surrender.

Cumque datum est nobis intelligi, quod quaedam personae inhabitantes praedictae villae et burgi de Notyngham post tempus praedictae praetensae sursum redditionis, suscipientes super se fore corpus corporatum per nomen 'Majoris, Aldermannorum, et Burgensium villae de Notyngham in Comitatu ejusdem villae' praetextu vel colore quarundam[2] literarum patentium per dictos nuper Reges Carolum et Jacobum Secundum[3] confectarum, diversas dimissiones vel praetensas dimissiones diversis personis diversarum terrarum, tenementorum, et hereditamentorum Majori et Burgensibus villae de Notyngham tempore praedictae praetensae sursum redditionis spectantium et pertinentium fecerunt, et diversas denariorum summas praetextu dictarum dimissionum vel praetensarum dimissionum habuerunt et receperunt; et quia nolumus, quod hujusmodi personae, quibus tales dimissiones vel praetensae dimissiones bona fide et pro valuabili consideratione factae fuerant, de hujusmodi firmis suis aliqualiter deprivari seu frustrari,[4] de gratia nostra speciali, ac ex certa scientia et mero motu nostris, concessimus et confirmavimus, ac per praesentes pro nobis, heredibus et successoribus nostris, concedimus et confirmamus omnibus et cuilibet

twentieth and of Scotland the fifty-sixth, or granted, or mentioned to be granted or confirmed, by any other the letters patent aforesaid to the Mayor and Burgesses of the town aforesaid, or which the Mayor and Burgesses of the town aforesaid, or their predecessors, by whatsoever name or names of incorporation, had, held, used or enjoyed, or occupied, or ought to have or might have had, held, used or enjoyed to them and to their successors before the said eighteenth day of September, in the abovesaid thirty-fourth year of the reign of the said late King Charles the Second, by reason or pretext of the aforesaid several letters patent, or of any one or more of them, or of other charters, grants, or letters patent whatsoever made, granted, or confirmed in any wise by any of our progenitors or ancestors late Kings or Queens of England before the said eighteenth day of September, in the thirty-fourth year of the said late King Charles the Second, or lawfully used, had, accustomed or enjoyed by other lawful manner, right, or title, custom, use or prescription whatsoever before the date of these presents.

<small>WILLIAM AND MARY.</small>

<small>or that they had before the pretended surrender.</small>

And whereas we are given to understand, that certain persons inhabitants of the aforesaid town and borough of Nottingham, after the time of the aforesaid surrender, taking upon themselves to be a body corporate by the name of 'the Mayor, Aldermen, and Burgesses of the town of Nottingham in the County of the same town,' under pretext or colour of certain letters patent made by the said late Kings Charles and James the Second, have made divers demises or pretended demises to divers persons of divers lands, tenements, and hereditaments belonging and pertaining to the Mayor and Burgesses of the town of Nottingham at the time of the aforesaid pretended surrender, and had and received divers sums of money under pretext of the said demises or pretended demises; and because we do not wish that such persons, to whom such demises and pretended demises were made in good faith and for valuable consideration, should be deceived or deprived in any wise of such their firms, we have, of our especial grace, and of our certain knowledge and mere motion, granted and confirmed,

<small>Confirmation of demises, etc., made by the pretended Council created after the pretended surrender.</small>

---

¹ *separalium*,] 'seperalium,' MS.   ² *quarundam*,] 'quorundam,' MS.
³ *Carolum . . . Secundum*,] 'Caroli Secundi et Jacobi Secundi,' MS.
⁴ *deprivari seu frustrari*.] So in MS.

WILLIAM AND MARY.

hujusmodi personae et personis, cui vel quibus aliquis talis dimissio vel praetensa dimissio, sive aliquae tales dimissiones vel praetensae dimissiones facta fuerat vel [factae] fuerant de aliquibus terris, tenementis, seu hereditamentis praedictis, quod quaelibet hujusmodi persona et personae deinceps respective habeant, teneant, et gaudeant, et habere, tenere, et gaudere possint et valeant omnia terras, tenementa, et hereditamenta eis vel eorum alicui vel aliquibus pro valuabili consideratione bona fide sic dimissa vel praetensa fore dimissa pro residuo respectivorum terminorum in qualibet hujusmodi dimissione limitatorum, sub annualibus redditibus, condicionibus, conventionibus, et agreamentis in hujusmodi dimissionibus specificatis, et juxta verum purportum dictarum dimissionum vel praetensarum dimissionum.

In cujus rei testimonium has literas nostras fieri fecimus patentes. Testibus nobis ipsis apud Westmonasterium, decimo nono die Octobris, anno regni nostri quarto.

Per Breve de Privato Sigillo.
Pigott.

Pro fine in Hanaperio viginti marcarum.   4182.

XXVIII.—*Grant of two Fairs by Queen Anne.*

1712, August 30.

QUEEN ANNE

ANNA, Dei gratia, Magnae Britanniae, Franciae, et Hiberniae Regina, Fidei Defensor, etc., omnibus, ad quos praesentes literae nostrae pervenerint, salutem.

Whereas it has been found by an inquisition that it would not be to our damage if we were to grant to the Burgesses of Nottingham two fairs;

Cum per quandam inquisitionem indentatam captam apud Guihald villae de Nottingham, in Comitatu nostro villae Nottingham, quinto die Maii, anno regni nostri undecimo, virtute cujusdam brevis nostri de *Ad quod Dampnum* e Cancellaria nostra nuper emanati, Vicecomitibus Comitatus villae Nottingham praedictae directi, et inquisitioni praedictae annexati, per sacramentum proborum et legalium hominum Comitatus praedicti, compertum sit, quod non esset ad aliquod dampnum vel praejudicium nostri aut aliorum, vel ad aliquod nocumentum vicinarum feriarum sive nundinarum, si nos concederemus Majori et Burgensibus villae de Nottingham praedictae, et successoribus suis, quod ipsi haberent et tenerent annuatim imperpetuum apud villam de Nottingham praedicta unam feriam

and we do by these presents for ourselves, our heirs and successors, grant and confirm to all and every such person and persons to whom any such demise or pretended demise, or any such demises or pretended demises has or have been made of any lands, tenements, or hereditaments aforesaid, that every such person and persons shall from henceforth respectively have, hold, and enjoy, and may and shall be able to have, hold, and enjoy all lands, tenements, and hereditaments so demised or pretended to be demised to them or to any of them for valuable consideration in good faith for the remainder of the respective terms limited in each such demise, under the annual rents, conditions, covenants, and agreements specified in such demises, and according to the true purport of the said demises or pretended demises.

In witness whereof we have caused these our letters to be made patent. Witness ourselves at Westminster, the nineteenth day of October, in the fourth year of our reign.

By writ of Privy Seal.
Pigott.

For a fine in the Hanaper of twenty marks.   4182.

WILLIAM AND MARY.

XXVIII.—*Grant of two Fairs by Queen Anne.*

1712, August 30.

ANNE, by the grace of God, of Great Britain, France, and Ireland Queen, Defender of the Faith, etc., to all to whom these our present letters shall come, greeting.

Whereas by an inquisition indented taken at the Gild Hall of the town of Nottingham, in the County of our town of Nottingham, on the fifth day of May, in the eleventh year of our reign, by virtue of a writ of ours of *Ad quod Dampnum* lately issued from our Chancery, addressed to the Sheriffs of the County of the town of Nottingham aforesaid, and annexed to the aforesaid inquisition, it was found by the oath of proved and lawful men of the County aforesaid, that it would not be any damage or prejudice to us or to others, or any injury to neighbouring fairs, if we were to grant to the Mayor and Burgesses of the town of Nottingham aforesaid, and to their successors, that they might have and hold yearly for ever at the

Marginal notes: QUEEN ANNE. Whereas it has been found by an inquisition that it would not be to our damage if we were to grant to the Burgesses of Nottingham two fairs;

QUEEN ANNE sive nundinam incipiendam in diem Jovis proximo ante festum Paschae, et tunc et ibidem tenendam et continuandam durantibus octo diebus tunc proximo sequentibus, et aliam feriam sive nundinam incipiendam in diem Veneris proximo praecedentem primum diem Martis immediate post festum Epiphaniae, tunc etiam tenendam et continuandam durantibus octo diebus tunc proximo sequentibus, pro emptione et venditione in feriis sive nundinis illis averiorum et pecorum ac omnium et omnimodorum bonorum, mercimoniorum, et mercandizarum quorumcunque communiter in feriis sive nundinis emptorum et venditorum, et tolneta et proficua inde provenientia et emergentia sibi et successoribus suis percipienda, prout per dicta breve et inquisitionem in filaciis Cancellariae nostrae praedictae de recordo remanentibus plenius liquet et apparet.

We do grant them two fairs of nine days each, Sciatis modo, quod nos, de gratia nostra speciali, ac ex certa scientia et mero motu nostris, dedimus et concessimus, ac per praesentes pro nobis, haeredibus et successoribus nostris, damus et concedimus praefatis Majori et Burgensibus villae de Nottingham praedicta, et successoribus suis, quod ipsi habeant et teneant annuatim imperpetuum apud villam de Nottingham

one on the Thursday before Easter, praedicta unam feriam sive nundinam incipiendam in diem Jovis proximo ante festum Paschae, et tunc et ibidem tenendam et continuandam durantibus octo diebus extunc proximo sequent-

and the other on Friday before the first Tuesday after Epiphany. ibus, et aliam feriam sive nundinam incipiendam in diem Veneris proximo praecedentem primum diem Martis immediate post festum Epiphaniae, tunc etiam tenendam et continuandam durantibus octo diebus extunc proximo sequentibus, pro emptione et venditione in feriis sive nundinis illis averiorum et pecorum ac omnium et omnimodorum bonorum, mercimoniorum, et mercandizarum quarumcunque communiter in feriis

Grant of Court of Pie-powder, tolls, etc. sive nundinis emptis et venditis, unacum Curia Pedis Pulverizati tempore feriarum praedictarum, ac cum omnibus tolnetis et aliis proficuis praedictis feriis sive nundinis pertinentibus sive spectantibus: habendas, tenendas, et gaudendas praedictas ferias sive nundinas et Curiam Pedis Pulverizati et caetera praemissa superius per praesentes concessa seu mentionata fore concessa eisdem Majori et Burgensibus villae de Nottingham praedicta, et successoribus suis, imperpetuum, ad solum et proprium opus et usum praefatorum Majoris et Burgensium villae de Nottingham

town of Nottingham aforesaid one fair to begin on the Thursday QUEEN ANNE
next before the feast of Easter, and then and there to be held
and continued during the eight days then next following, and
another fair to begin on Friday next preceding the first Tuesday
immediately after the feast of Epiphany, then also to be held
and continued during eight days then next following, for buying
and selling in these fairs of cattle and sheep and of all and all
manner goods, merceries, and merchandize whatsoever commonly
bought and sold in fairs, and to take toll and the profits thence
happening and arising to them and to their successors, as by
the said writ and inquisition remaining of record in the files of
our Chancery more fully appears and is made evident.

Know ye therefore, that we, of our especial grace, and of our We do grant
certain knowledge and mere motion, have given and granted, them two
and do by these presents for us, our heirs and successors, give fairs of nine
and grant to the aforesaid Mayor and Burgesses of the town of days each,
Nottingham aforesaid, and to their successors, that they may
have and hold annually for ever at the town of Nottingham
aforesaid a fair beginning on the Thursday next before the feast one on the
of Easter, and then and there to be held and continued during Thursday be-
the eight days then next following, and another fair to begin fore Easter,
on the Friday next preceding the first Tuesday immediately and the other
after the feast of Epiphany, then also to be held and continued on Friday
during the eight days then next following, for the buying and before the
selling in those fairs of cattle and sheep and of all and all first Tuesday
manner of goods, merceries, and merchandize whatsoever com- after Epi-
monly bought and sold in fairs, together with a Court of phany.
Piepowder in the time of the fair aforesaid, and with all tolls
and other profits pertaining or belonging to the aforesaid fairs: Grant of Court
to have, hold, and enjoy the aforesaid fairs and Court of Pie- of Piepowder and the other premises above by these presents granted powder,
or mentioned to be granted to the same Mayor and Burgesses tolls, etc.
of the town of Nottingham aforesaid, and to their successors, for
ever, for the sole and proper use and behoof of the aforesaid
Mayor and Burgesses of the town of Nottingham aforesaid, and
of their successors, and this without rendering, paying, or

Queen Anne praedicta, et successorum suorum, et hoc absque compoto vel aliquo alio nobis, haeredibus vel successoribus nostris, proinde reddendo, solvendo, vel faciendo.

Enactment clause.
Quare volumus, ac per praesentes pro nobis, haeredibus et successoribus nostris, firmiter injungendo praecipimus et mandamus, quod praefati Major et Burgenses villae de Nottingham praedicta, et successores sui, vigore praesentium bene, libere, licite, et quiete habeant, teneant, et custodiant, et habere, tenere, et custodire valeant et possint imperpetuum praedictas ferias sive nundinas, unacum Curia Pedis Pulverizati et caeteris praemissis praedictis, secundum tenorem et veram intentionem harum literarum nostrarum patentium absque molestatione, perturbatione, gravamine, sive contradictione nostri, haeredum vel successorum nostrorum, vel aliquorum Vicecomitum, escaetorum, ballivorum, officiariorum, sive ministrorum nostrorum, haeredum vel successorum nostrorum quorumcunque; et hoc absque aliquo alio warranto, brevi, vel processu imposterum in ea parte procurando vel obtinendo.

Denique volumus, ac per praesentes pro nobis, haeredibus et successoribus nostris, concedimus praefatis Majori et Burgensibus villae de Nottingham praedicta, et successoribus suis, quod hae literae nostrae patentes vel irrotulamentum earundem sint et erunt bonum, firmum, validum, sufficiens, et effectuale in lege eisdem Majori et Burgensibus villae de Nottingham praedicta, et successoribus suis, secundum veram intentionem earundem.

In cujus rei testimonium has literas nostras fieri fecimus patentes. Teste me ipsa, apud Westmonasterium, tricesimo die Augusti, anno regni nostri undecimo.

Per breve de Privato Sigillo.
Cocks.
4183.

making any account or anything else therefor to us, our heirs or successors. {Queen Anne}

Wherefore we will, and do by these presents for us, our heirs and successors, firmly enjoining command and order that the aforesaid Mayor and Burgesses of the town of Nottingham aforesaid, and their successors, may, by force of these presents, well, fully, lawfully, and quietly have, hold, and keep, and may and shall be able to have, hold, and keep for ever the aforesaid fairs, together with a Court of Piepowder and the other premises aforesaid, according to the tenor and true intent of these our letters patent without molestation, perturbation, grievance, or contradiction of us, our heirs or successors, or of any Sheriffs, escheators, bailiffs, officers, or ministers of us, our heirs or successors whatsoever; and this without any other warrant, writ, or process to be hereafter procured or obtained in this behalf. {Enactment clause.}

Finally we will, and do by these presents for us, our heirs and successors, grant to the aforesaid Mayor and Burgesses of the town of Nottingham aforesaid, and to their successors, that these our letters patent and the enrolment of the same may and shall be good, firm, valid, sufficient, and effectual in law for the same Mayor and Burgesses of the town of Nottingham aforesaid, and their successors, according to the true intent of the same.

In witness whereof we have caused these our letters to be made patent. Witness myself, at Westminster, the thirtieth day of August, in the eleventh year of our reign.

By writ of Privy Seal.
Cocks.
4183.

ANALYTICAL INDEX.

Aldermen, power to elect seven, Henry VI., p. 62; [Charles II., p. 90].
    to hold office for life, Henry VI., p. 64; [Charles II., p. 98].
    amovable by the Burgesses, Henry VI., p. 64.
    to be Justices of the Peace, Henry VI., p. 64.
    may wear gowns, hoods, and cloaks of one suit, as the Aldermen of London do, Henry VI., p. 68.

Ale, forfeited, granted to the Burgesses, Henry VI., p. 66.

Amercements, from all men and tenants in the borough in all Courts granted to the Burgesses, Henry IV., p. 40; amplified, Henry VI., p. 60.
    imposed by Justices of the Peace granted to the Burgesses, Henry IV., p. 44.

Array, Commissions of, Mayor to be joined to all, relating to the borough, Henry IV., p. 44.

Assize, Pleas of, grant of cognizance of all, relating to tenures within the borough, Henry IV., p. 40.

Bail. *See* Mainpernors.

Bailiffs, two to be elected, one for each borough of the town, Edward I., p. 20.
    may be elected where most convenient, owing to the poverty of one of the boroughs of the town; Edward III., p. 32.
    grant of power to elect two Sheriffs in place of the two Bailiffs, Henry VI., p. 52.
    See also Reeve.

Borough, all residents within, to contribute to tallages, etc., like the burgesses, Henry II., p. 4; John, Earl of Mortain, p. 6; King John, p. 10.
    freedom obtained by residence of a year and day within, Henry II., p. 2; John, Earl of Mortain, p. 6; King John, p. 8.
    liberties of, seized into King's hands and restored, Edward I., p. 18; Edward III., p. 26.
    pleas arising within the borough not to be pleaded out of the borough, Edward II., p. 22.

Borough—*continued.*
    Sheriffs, officers, etc., of the King excluded from entering the borough, Edward II., p. 24.
    incorporation of, Henry VI., p. 50; recital that the town had been previously incorporated under a certain form, *ibid.*
    created a County, Henry VI., p. 52.

Borough Court. *See* Court.

Boroughs of the town, two, a Bailiff to be elected in each of the, owing to the different customs prevailing in them, Edward I., p. 20; grant of permission to elect the two Bailiffs where most convenient, owing to the poverty of one of the two boroughs, Edward III., p. 32.

Burgesses not to be arrested elsewhere for debts of other Burgesses of Nottingham, unless the Burgesses have failed to do justice to the creditors, Henry III., pp. 14, 16.
    not to be impleaded out of the borough concerning tenements in the borough, Edward II., p. 22.
    not to be joined with strangers in assizes, juries, or inquests relating to any matters outside the borough, Edward II., p. 24.
    to make all assizes, juries, and inquests relating to the borough within the borough, foreigners being excluded from all such inquests, etc., Edward II., p. 24.
    acquittance of, from various tolls, imposts, etc., Edward II., p. 24; Edward III., p. 30.
    exempted from jurisdiction of the Steward and Marshall of the Royal Household, Henry VI., p. 66.

Castle, the, exempted from the County of the town, Henry VI., p. 52.

Chamberlains, power to elect two, [Charles II., pp. 92, 104].

Chattels, forfeited, of felons and fugitives of the tenants and residents within the borough, granted to the Burgesses, Henry IV., p. 40.

Clerk, Common, power to elect a, [Charles II., pp. 110, 112].
    to be approved by the King, [Charles II., p. 114; James II., p. 128].

Cloths, working of dyed, restricted to borough, Henry II., p. 2; John, Earl of Mortain, p. 6; King John, p. 8.

Coroners to be elected by the Burgesses, Henry III., p. 12.
    to administer oath of office to the Escheator, Henry VI., p. 60.
    power to elect two, [Charles II., p. 106].

Councillors, Chief, power to elect 18, [Charles II., pp. 90, 100].
Councillors, Common, power to elect 6, [Charles II., pp. 92, 102].
    power to elect 18, William and Mary, p. 134.
County, the borough created a, Henry VI., p. 52.
County Hall (King's Hall) exempted from the County of the town, Henry VI., p. 52.
Court of Borough, Mayor and Bailiffs to hear all pleas relating to lands, tenements, trespasses, contracts, etc., within the borough, Edward II., p. 24; grant of cognizance of all pleas relating to lands, tenements, trespasses, covenants, plaints, etc., of all tenants and residents within the borough, to be held before the Mayor and Bailiffs, Henry IV., p. 38.
    grant of cognizance of pleas of assize relating to tenures within the borough, Henry IV., p. 40.
    powers of Borough Court defined, Henry VI., p. 56.
    to be held in the Gildhall before the Mayor and Sheriffs, Henry VI., p. 58.
    profits arising from, granted to the Burgesses, Henry VI., p. 58.
    See also Justices of the Peace.

Deodands granted to the Burgesses, Henry VI., p. 60.

Escheator, the Mayor to be, Henry VI., p. 54.
    no other Escheator but the Mayor to be made for the borough, Henry VI., p. 56.
    permission to make his proffer and account annually at the Exchequer by attorney, Henry VI., pp. 58, 68; shall not be compelled to attend personally at the Exchequer to render his accounts, *idem,* p. 60.
    Oath of office of, to be taken before the Coroners, Henry VI., p. 60; the Escheator not to be compelled to come out of the borough to take his oath of office, *ibid.*
    name of, to be certified into the Chancery within twelve days of the election of Mayor, Henry VI., p. 60.

Fair, Epiphany, fair of eight days beginning on the Friday before the first Tuesday before Epiphany, Anne, p. 142.

Fair—*continued.*

> St. Peter in Cathedra, feast of (Feb. 22), grant of a fair of fifteen days at, in place of the fair at the feast of St. Edmund (Nov. 20), Richard II., p. 34.
>
> St. Matthias (Feb. 24), abolished, [Charles II., p. 116; restored, James II., p. 124].
>
> Easter, fair of eight days beginning on the Thursday before Easter, Anne, p. 142.
>
> April 23, fair of eight days at, grant of, [Charles II., p. 116; abolished, James II., p. 124].
>
> St. Matthew, feast of (Sept. 21), of eight days, confirmed, Edward I., p. 20; [restored, James II., p. 124].
>
> November 1, fair of eight days at, grant of, [Charles II., p. 116; abolished, James II., p. 124].
>
> St. Edmund, feast of (Nov. 20), of fifteen days, grant of, Edward I., p. 20; changed to a fair at the feast of St. Peter in Cathedra (Feb. 22), Richard II., p. 34.

Fee-ferm of the Borough, to be paid by the Reeve into the Exchequer, John, Earl of Mortain, p. 6; King John, p. 10; to be paid into the Exchequer at two terms by the Burgesses' own hands, Henry III., p. 12.

> described as £52 *blanc*, Henry III., p. 12; Edward I., p. 18.
>
> increment of £8 added to, Edward I., p. 18.

Felones de se, disavowed chattels of, granted to the Burgesses, Henry VI., p. 60.

Felons, forfeited chattels of, granted to the Burgesses, Henry IV., p. 40; amplified, Henry VI., p. 60.

Fines for trespasses and offences, of all men and residents of the borough, in all Courts, granted to the Burgesses, Henry IV., p. 40; amplified, Henry VI., p. 60.

> post fines (fines *pro licentia concordandi*) of all men and residents of the borough granted to the Burgesses, Henry IV., p. 40; Henry VI., p. 60.
>
> imposed by the Justices of the Peace granted to the Burgesses, Henry IV., p. 44; amplified, Henry VI., p. 66; the Escheator and Sheriffs not to account at the Exchequer for, Henry VI., p. 68.
>
> profits arising from Borough Court granted to the Burgesses, Henry VI., p. 58.
>
> from all sureties and mainpernors granted to the Burgesses, Henry VI., p. 62.

Forfeitures. Chattels of felons and fugitives of the tenants and residents within the borough granted to the Burgesses, Henry IV., p. 40; amplified, Henry VI., p. 60.
    grant of forfeitures, etc., of all men and tenants in the borough, Henry IV., p. 40.
    from all pledges and mainpernors granted to the Burgesses, Henry VI., p. 62.
    of victuals and ale granted to the Burgesses, Henry VI., p. 66.

Freedom, obtained by residence of a year and a day within the borough, Henry II., p. 2; John, Earl of Mortain, p. 6; King John, p. 8.

Fugitives, chattels of, granted to the Burgesses, Henry IV., p. 40.

Gaol, Borough, recital that the Burgesses have one by prescription, Edward III., p. 28.
    confirmation of right to have, Edward III., p. 30.

Household, Royal, the Steward and Marshal of the, not to sit in the town, Henry VI., pp. 58, 66.

Incorporation of the borough, which had been long a town incorporated under a certain form, Henry VI., p. 50; [Charles II., p. 88].

Infangenetheof, grant of, Henry II., p. 2; John, Earl of Mortain, p. 4; King John, p. 8.

Inquests, juries, etc., relating to the borough to be taken by Burgesses only, Edward II., p. 24.

Issues, forfeited, of all men and tenants in the borough, granted to the Burgesses, Henry IV., p. 40; amplified, Henry VI., p. 60.

Juries relating to the borough to be empanelled of Burgesses only, Edward II., p. 24.

Jurisdiction, pleas relating to tenements, trespasses, etc., within the borough not to be pleaded out of the borough, Edward II., p. 22.
    grant of cognizance of all pleas relating to lands, tenements, trespasses, covenants, plaints, etc., of all tenants and residents within the borough, to be held before the Mayor and Bailiffs, Henry IV., p. 38.

Jurisdiction—*continued.*
>grant of cognizance of pleas of assize relating to tenures within the borough, Henry IV., p. 40.
>of Justices of the Peace, Henry IV., p. 44.
>of Borough Court defined, Henry VI., p. 56.

Justices of the Peace. The Mayor, Recorder, and four others to be elected by the Mayor to hear and determine all pleas, etc., pertaining to the offices of Justices of the Peace, Justices of Labourers and Artizans, Henry IV., p. 44; amplified, Henry VI., p. 64.
>grant of all fines, profits, etc., arising from the jurisdiction of, to the Burgesses, Henry IV., p. 44; amplified, Henry VI., p. 66.
>Aldermen to be, Henry VI., p. 64.
>jurisdiction of, defined, Henry VI., p. 64.

King's Sheriffs or officers excluded from interfering with the service of writs or levying distraints, within the borough, or from entering the same, Henry III., p. 16 *bis*; amplified, Edward II., p. 24; Edward III., p. 28; Henry IV., p. 42.

Land, power for the Mayor and Burgesses to acquire, Henry VI., p. 52; [Charles II., p. 88].
>unchallenged possession of, for a year and a day, sufficient title, Henry II., p. 2; John, Earl of Mortain, p. 6; King John, p. 10.

Lastage, Burgesses exempt from payment of, Edward II., p. 24.

Liberties not to be forfeited for non-user, Edward II., p. 22; Henry IV., p. 38.
>seised into the King's hands and restored to the Burgesses, Edward I., p. 18; Edward III., p. 26.
>to be enjoyed by the Burgesses in as ample manner as any of their predecessors enjoyed them, Henry IV., p. 46.

Mainpernors, fines and issues from, granted to the Burgesses, Henry VI., p. 62.

Markets, Friday and Saturday, Henry II., p. 2; John, Earl of Mortain, p. 4; King John, p. 8.
>Saturday, confirmation of, Edward III., p. 30.
>—— persons attending, exempt from distraint, except for the King's ferm, Henry II., p. 4; John, Earl of Mortain, p. 6; King John, p. 10.

ANALYTICAL INDEX. 153

Mayor, creation of office of, Edward I., p. 20.

    election of, manner of, Edward I., p. 20; [Charles II., pp. 90, 94].

    Mayor and Bailiffs to hold court for all pleas relating to lands, trespasses, contracts, etc., within the borough, Edward II., p. 24.

    Mayor, Recorder and four others to be elected by the Mayor to hear and determine all pleas, etc., pertaining to the offices of Justices of the Peace, Justices of Labourers and Artizans, Henry IV., p. 44; amplified, Henry VI., p. 64.

    to be joined to all Commissions of Array in the borough, Henry IV., p. 44.

    Sheriffs to take oaths of office before, Henry VI., p. 52.

    to be Escheator of the borough, Henry VI., p. 54.

    to be one of the Aldermen, Henry VI., p. 64.

    Deputy, the Mayor may appoint a, [Charles II., p. 96].

Merchants' Gild, grant of, John, Earl of Mortain, p. 6; King John, p. 10.

Murage, Burgesses exempt from payment of, Edward II., p. 24.

Murder (fines for), of all men and tenants of the borough granted to the Burgesses, Henry IV., p. 40.

Non-user, liberties exempt from forfeiture for, Edward II., p. 22; Henry IV., p. 38.

Office, refusal to accept, power to inflict fine for, [Charles II., p. 108].

Outlaws, chattels of, granted to the Burgesses, Henry VI., p. 60.

Passage, Burgesses exempt from payment of, Edward II., p. 24.

Pavage, Burgesses exempt from payment of, Edward II., p. 24.

Pleas, grant of cognizance of all, relating to lands, tenements, trespasses, covenants, etc., within the borough, Edward II., p. 22; amplified, Henry IV., p. 38.

    of assize relating to tenures within the borough, grant of cognizance of, Henry IV., p. 40.

    relating to tenements, trespasses, contracts, etc., within the borough not to be pleaded outside the borough, but to be pleaded before the Mayor and Bailiffs, Edward II., p. 24.

Pledges, fines and forfeitures from, granted to the Burgesses, Henry VI., p. 62.
Pontage, Burgesses exempt from payment of, Edward III., p. 30.
Purprestures, grant to the Burgesses of licence to approve themselves of all, Henry IV., p. 42.

Quayage, Burgesses exempt from payment of, Edward II., p. 24.

Ransoms of all men and tenants in the borough granted to the Burgesses, Henry IV., p. 40; amplified, Henry VI., p. 60.
Recorder on the Commission of the Peace, Henry IV., p. 44.
    power to elect a, [Charles II., pp. 108, 112].
    Deputy, power for Recorder to appoint a, [Charles II., p. 112].
    to be approved by the Crown, [Charles II., p. 114; James II., p. 128].
Reeve of borough, cannot prosecute a Burgess unless another Burgess is prosecutor, Henry II., p. 2; John, Earl of Mortain, p. 2; King John, p. 10.
    burgesses may elect their own, John, Earl of Mortain, p. 6; King John, p. 10.
    removable at King's pleasure, John, Earl of Mortain, p. 6; King John, p. 10.
    to pay the fee-ferm of the borough into the Exchequer at the two terms of the Exchequer, John, Earl of Mortain, p. 6; King John, p. 10.
    See also Bailiffs.
Return of Writs, grant of, Henry III., pp. 14, 16; amplified, Edward II., p. 24; Edward III., p. 28; Henry IV., p. 42.

Seal, Common, the Mayor and Burgesses to have a, [Charles II., p. 90].
Sheriffs (of town), grant of power to elect two, in place of the two Bailiffs, Henry VI., p. 52.
    to hold office for one year, Henry VI., p. 54.
    oaths of office of, to be taken before the Mayor, and not outside the borough, Henry VI., p. 54.
    names of, to be certified into Chancery, Henry VI., p. 54.
    no other Sheriffs for the town to be made, Henry VI., p. 56.
    writs formerly addressed to the Sheriffs of the County to be addressed to the Sheriffs of the town, Henry VI., p. 56.
    County Courts to be held monthly by, Henry VI., p. 56.

Sheriffs (of town)—*continued.*
    may make their proffers and accounts at the Exchequer annually by attornies, Henry VI., pp. 58, 66; the Sheriffs not to be forced to attend in person at the Exchequer to render their account, *ibid.*

Sheriffs (of County) excluded from interfering with the service of writs or levying distraints within the borough, Henry III., p. 16 *bis*; amplified, Edward II., p. 24; Edward III., p. 28; Henry IV., p. 42.
    writs formerly addressed to, to be addressed to the Sheriffs of the town, Henry VI., p. 56.

Stallage, Burgesses exempt from payment of, Edward II., p. 24.

Statutes Merchant, the Common Clerk to take and enrol, [Charles II., p. 110].

Sureties, fines and forfeitures from, granted to the Burgesses, Henry VI., p. 62.

Terrage, Burgesses exempt from payment of, Edward II., p. 24.

Theam, grant of, Henry II., p. 2; John, Earl of Mortain, p. 4; King John, p. 8.

Thelonea, grant of, Henry II., p. 2; John, Earl of Mortain, p. 4; King John, p. 8.

Tol, grant of, Hen. II., p. 2; John, Earl of Mortain, p. 4; King John, p. 8.

Tolls, acquittance of burgesses from, John, Earl of Mortain, p. 6; King John, p. 10.

Town Clerk. *See* Clerk, Common.

Trent, rights of Burgesses over, throughout county, Henry II., p. 2; John, Earl of Mortain, p. 4; King John, p. 8.
    passage of, free to navigators for one perch on each side of the thread of the stream, Hen. II., p. 4; John, Earl of Mortain, p. 6; King John, p. 10.

Tronage, grant of, within borough, Henry III., p. 12.

Victuals, forfeited, granted to the Burgesses, Henry VI., p. 66.

Wastes, grant to the Burgesses of licence to approve themselves of, Henry IV., p. 42.

Wine, forfeited, granted to the Burgesses, Henry VI., p. 66.

Year, day, waste, and estrepment, of all men and tenants in the borough granted to the burgesses, Henry IV., p. 40.

www.ingramcontent.com/pod-product-compliance
Lightning Source LLC
Chambersburg PA
CBHW030258170426
43202CB00009B/794